Depression Glass
Collections and Reflections

DEPRESSION GLASS
Collections and Reflections

A Guide With Values

Doris Yeske

4880 Lower Valley Road, Atglen, PA 19310 USA

To my loyal and supportive family and friends who gave me the encouragement, enthusiasm, and immense support that I needed to write this second book on Depression Glass, the highly collectible glassware that collectors search for today. Their infinite patience and interest in hunting for additional patterns, rare pieces, premium giveaways, and information on this popular glassware is deeply appreciated.

Copyright © 1999 by Doris Yeske
Library of Congress Catalog Card Number: 98-83141

All rights reserved. No part of this work may be reproduced or used in any form or by any means—graphic, electronic, or mechanical, including photocopying or information storage and retrieval systems—without written permission from the copyright holder.
"Schiffer," "Schiffer Publishing Ltd. & Design," and the "Design of pen and ink well" are registered trademarks of Schiffer Publishing Ltd.

Designed by "Sue"
Type set in Berhard Modern BT/
Souvenir Lt BT

ISBN: 0-7643-0838-6
Printed in China
1 2 3 4

Published by Schiffer Publishing Ltd.
4880 Lower Valley Road
Atglen, PA 19310
Phone: (610) 593-1777;
Fax: (610) 593-2002
E-mail: Schifferbk@aol.com
Please visit our web site catalog at
www.schifferbooks.com

This book may be purchased
from the publisher.
Include $3.95 for shipping.
Please try your bookstore first.
We are interested in hearing from authors
with book ideas on related subjects.
You may write for a free catalog.

In Europe, Schiffer books are distributed
by
Bushwood Books
6 Marksbury Rd.
Kew Gardens
Surrey TW9 4JF England
Phone: 44 (0)181 392-8585; Fax: 44
(0)181 392-9876
E-mail: Bushwd@aol.com

CONTENTS

ACKNOWLEDGMENTS

Many people have assisted me in the preparation of this book. Again, my dedicated family with their enormous concern, assistance, and inspiration has been invaluable in writing this second book.

A very special thanks to my instructor and classmates for their sincere interest and willingness to share their thoughts with me. I value their loyalty and friendship.

I wish to acknowledge my two photographers, Caroline Martinez of Tomah, Wisconsin, for coming into my home and spending hours in the selection, arrangement, and photographing of my glassware, and Joseph Photographers of Portland, Oregon, who artistically arranged and photographed many additional pieces including rare glassware. Without their technical expertise I would not have been able to complete this book. I am deeply indebted to both individuals for their excellent work.

I am especially grateful to my daughter Karen and son-in-law Mark who provided the glassware from their extensive collection for the photographers in addition to their technical writing and editing suggestions.

A special thanks to my friends Ted and Cathy Ostrowski and their sons Teddy and Tyler for providing me with the pieces of glassware that I needed for special photographs.

A special acknowledgment to my friend Betty Wish of La Crosse, Wisconsin for reading the entire manuscript and making valuable suggestions.

I am deeply indebted to my daughters Cheryl and Sharon, who did an extraordinary, time-consuming job of preparing the manuscript.

A special acknowledgment to my friend Joan M. Anderson of La Crosse, Wisconsin, who did the typing of the photo identifications.

The aid and advice given by many depression glass collectors and dealers have proven to be highly significant in writing this book.

PREFACE

This book will appeal to both collectors and non-collectors, as it adds a new dimension, a sparkle, to the collecting of Depression Glass, today's number one collectible.

Collectors need not only a price guide but also a comprehensive background of this glassware. In a detailed manner, therefore, I have tried to provide the basic history and memories of the Great Depression. Very significant is the origin of the glassware, the numerous patterns, the array of bold and beautiful colors, the popular sources of collecting, the companies that produced this glassware, and the increasing popularity.

Depression Glass has become one of the hottest areas of interest on the Internet. This book, containing the basics and current value of this distinctive glassware, will be indispensable to any collector. The need for preservation of this highly coveted glassware, which is becoming more and more relevant, is also stressed in the book.

INTRODUCTION

Since the publication of my first book, *Depression Glass, A Collector's Guide*, so much enthusiasm and interest has been generated among readers about the history of the Depression Era and the colored glassware produced that I decided to write and share more information on this popular glassware.

My down-to-earth style of providing separate chapters on specific subjects, followed with pictures, detailed descriptions, information on popular companies with dates, and the pricing of this historical glassware will appeal to all collectors of this fast growing hobby.

Depression Glass as a collectible has mushroomed so quickly, in spite of the increasing scarcity and soaring prices, that now more than ever collectors need to be increasingly knowledgeable in their search for this unforgettable colored glassware.

Since so many new collectors are becoming enthralled with Depression Glass, this book offers invaluable collector's advice and accurate prices. Two chapters in particular, "What Collectors Should Know" and "Update On Reproductions," are extremely useful now that reproductions are becoming the main pitfalls of collecting Depression Glass.

It is my wish that this book will assist any collector to collect more wisely and to appreciate these precious artifacts.

Price Guide

Prices listed here are for glass in mint condition, meaning no chips, cracks, flakes, and extreme wear marks. If present, these will definitely affect the price by 50 percent or more. The price on a rare item may be reduced by 25 percent and probably more, depending upon the amount of damage done. These prices are only a guide due to regional differences which determine the supply and demand. The prices listed here are the prices found in antique shops, shows, flea markets, and from various dealers located in the midwest. The dealers have a tremendous impact upon the determination of the prices.

UNFORGETTABLE EVENTS AND MEMORIES OF THE GREAT DEPRESSION

Growing up in the Depression in the 1920s and 1930s there were so many unforgettable and memorable events that brought about so many changes in the lifestyle of most families. With the crash of the stock market in 1929, banks closed, factories shut down, farmers lost their farms, unemployment was experienced everywhere, and nature dealt its worst blows; nonetheless, the people strove to go on. During this bad period, life had to go on and families tried to observe and take in as many of the activities they could to enlighten their lives. If there was ever a time when the people needed and could use a little excitement in their lives, it was during these years.

Place Setting, Cameo, "Ballerina" or "Dancing Girl," Hocking Glass Co., 1930-1934. One of Hocking's first mold etched, popular and attractive patterns for novice collectors to identify. Interesting is the human figure as part of the laced on decoration. Little dancing girls with long draped scarves appear in the borders of the plates and are surrounded by festoons and ribbon bows. **Back row left to right:** sugar, 3-1/4", $18; creamer, 3-1/4", $22; cup, $8; saucer, 6", $3. **Center:** plate, 9-1/2", $9, yellow.

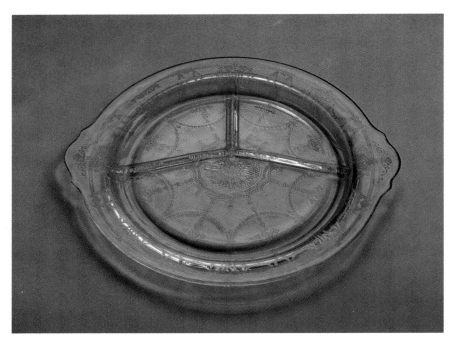

Plate, Cameo, "Ballerina" or "Dancing Girl" by Hocking. Grill with closed handles, $6, yellow.

Remember the catalogues, the popular means of communication and entertainment? I especially remember Sears and Roebuck. Sets of the colored glassware produced during this era could be ordered from this well known catalogue. It was fun just browsing through the catalogues and looking forward to the new issues. Store windows too would display this glittering glassware in yellow, green, and pink.

Who can forget the world and county fairs? The Pittsburgh Glass Exhibit, the famous and single biggest glass event of every year, was a big boost to the glass industry, which was then producing the colored glassware. The buildings were filled with various glassmakers and glass buyers. Pittsburgh was the popular show to which glassmakers came from various states to display their new lines to the buyers. Exhibits were huge and spectacular, with room after room of brilliant glassware. People wanted their lives more colorful and this annual event certainly proved it. The World's Fair in Chicago in 1933, perhaps the greatest show in the world as many recall, had fabulous exhibits of colored glassware. It was a godsend that helped the people there find jobs and regain some pride.

The county fairs were an annual event that young adults looked forward to. Seeing the various rides, numerous exhibits, and people for miles around gave everyone an exhilarating feeling. The numerous booths of games where you could toss pennies—if you had them—into vases, bowls, and tumblers of yellow, pink, green, and red was a popular form of entertainment. If you were lucky, you'd receive one of these beautiful pieces, a treasured prize.

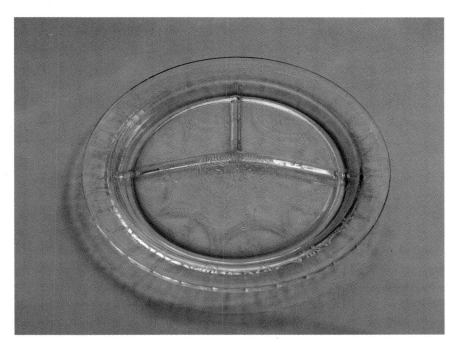

Plate, Cameo, "Ballerina" or "Dancing Girl" by Hocking. Grill, 10-1/2", $6, yellow.

Place Setting, Cameo, "Ballerina" or "Dancing Girl" by Hocking in green. Plate, 9-1/2", dinner, $20; cup, $15; saucer, 6", $4.

Plate, Cameo, "Ballerina" or "Dancing Girl" by Hocking. Plate, 10-1/2", with closed handles, $12, green. These sets were widely distributed by Sears and Roebuck Co.

For adults, a big night out meant going to the movies. Attending the movies for 30 to 40 cents was where one could escape reality for a couple of hours. For housewives, the best part of going to the movies was receiving a different colored dish one night a week. Hundreds of women crowded into the local movies weekly to receive a free cup, saucer, dinner plate, butter dish, or platter to compete their dinnerware. What a thrill it must have been to build this set, the colored glassware known as Depression Glass. This, as we well remember, became known as "Dish Night." It may have been just as entertaining as seeing the glamorous movie stars: Shirley Temple, Fred Astaire, Ginger Rogers, Gary Cooper, Tyrone Power, John Wayne, Errol Flynn and others.

The radio was everywhere in its heyday. This, too, was a great source of entertainment, with famous radio personalities who had nearly everyone glued to the radio. Remember Horace Heidt and his Musical Knights featuring his triple-tongued trumpets?

The 4th of July, a very memorable event in the '30s, mixed patriotism and fun. It was truly the old fashioned Independence Day. Flags were displayed all over, especially a large one on the porch roof. The car that I polished for a whole day had small flags displayed on the hood. Again, the memorable colors of red, white, and blue played a big part in this drab period. The highlight of the day was a picnic lunch served in green and pink Depression Glass. I can recall the pitcher containing lemonade sitting in the middle of the table. What a colorful looking table with the very best of goodies! Watching the parade (another colorful event), displaying the flags, and singing patriotic songs were all very entertaining.

Yes, there was gloom and doom in this era but there were the activities described above plus a few more that brightened people's lives and brought them out of the doldrums.

Floral and Diamond Band, U.S. Glass Co., late 1920s. This is a heavy pressed type of glassware in a molded flower design, sharply cut and resembling cut glass. This set was advertised by Sears and Roebuck. There are variations in the color green. **Back row left to right:** sherbet, $8; plate, 8", luncheon, $45; compote, 5-1/2" tall, $18. **Bottom row left to right:** bowl, 5-3/4", handled, $12; bowl, 4-1/2", berry, $9.

Tumbler, Rose Cameo, Belmont, 1931. This pattern resembles Cameo except for the encircled rose in the decorated border. A limited number of pieces were made. Tumbler, 5", ftd., $22.

Setting, Sharon, "Cabbage Rose," Federal Glass Co., 1935-1939. This was a very popular pattern back in the 1930s and was widely distributed by Sears and Roebuck. Many collectors seem to begin collecting with a few pieces of this pattern. Many had this as the primary dinner set. Very attractive with center motif of a curved spray of roses with spokes on the border. **Left to right:** sugar, ftd., $14; plate, 6", $8; creamer, ftd., $18; bowl, 5", cream soup, $50.

Display of glassware exhibited at the World's Fairs, Pittsburgh and Chicago. **Left to right:** sherbet, Craquel, $4; sherbet, Madrid, $11; plate, Patrician, "Spoke," $12; tumbler, Georgian, $8; sugar, Homespun, "Fine Rib," $10. **Center:** swan, $22.

Display of glassware exhibited at the World's Fairs. **Left to right:** sherbet, Normandie, "Bouquet and Lattice," $7; tumbler, "Windsor Diamond," $12; plate, 9", Georgian, "Love Birds," $8; tumbler, cobalt blue, $10; bowl, 4-1/2", Royal Ruby, $6. **Center:** candy dish, 8", low tab handles, Old Cafe, $12.

Display of glassware exhibited at the World's Fairs. **Left to right:** sherbet, 4-3/4", ftd., Ring, "Banded Rings," $5; plate, 8", luncheon, Twisted Optic, $4; sherbet, Florentine No. 2, "Poppy No. 2," $11; cup, Florentine No. 1, "Poppy No. 1," $9.

Display of glassware exhibited at the World's Fairs. **Left to right:** bowl, Sandwich, 5" to 5-1/2", $12; sherbet, ftd., Royal Ruby, $9; creamer, Newport "Hairpin," $13; coaster, $6.

Display of glassware exhibited at World's Fairs. **Left to right:** sherbet, $3; tumbler, Hex Optic, "Honeycomb," $5; sugar, Sharon, "Cabbage Rose," $15; bowl, Spiral, $5.

Glassware from county fairs. **Left to right:** bowl, Oyster and Pearl, $25; vase, cobalt blue, $25; tumbler, "Bow Knot," $23; sherbet, Lorain Basket, No. 615, $33; bowl, Fortune, $9.

Weekly movie, "Dish Night." Attending a movie was a great weekly event, especially for the housewives who received a free colored bowl. If you attended the movie every week you could receive a free cup, saucer, dinner plate, cereal bowl, cake, and torte plate. This was the beginning of building the set of colored glassware known as Depression Glass. **Left to right:** bowl, large, 7-1/8", berry, U.S. Swirl, $15; bowl, 9", vegetable, Cremax, MacBeth-Evans, $15; bowl, 8-1/4", large berry, Waterford "Waffle," $25.

Weekly additions. Plate, 11-1/2", sandwich, Cremax, decorated with pink, $12.

Weekly additions. **Left to right:** bowl, 5-3/4", cereal, decal decorated, $8; cup, decal decorated, $6; saucer, decal decorated, $3; plate, 9-3/4", dinner, Cremax, $10.

Weekly additions. Plate, 11-1/2", sandwich, Cremax, decal decorated, $13.

Weekly addition. Plate, 13-3/4", sandwich, Waterford "Waffle," $28, scarce.

Weekly additions. Plate, 10-1/4", handled cake, Waterford "Waffle," $18; plate, 9-5/8", dinner, $25, scarce.

Picnic lunch served in brilliant pink. Coronation, "Banded Fine Rib," "Saxon," Hocking Glass Co., 1936-1940. A plain pattern with the plates having a narrow sunburst of radial lines surrounded by larger, more widely spaced lines. The border has an inner circle of ridges with a plain outer band. **Left to right:** cup, $6; bowl, large, 8", berry, $9; sherbet, $5; plate, 8-1/2", luncheon, $5.

Picnic lunch served in green, Spiral, Hocking Glass Co., 1928-1930. Produced only in green. Plates have plain centers and wide borders have swirled lines going toward the left, or clockwise, in a pinwheel effect. **Left to right:** plate, 8", luncheon, $4; sherbet, $4; cup, $5; saucer, $2.

Popular pitcher produced in the 1930s for serving drinks. Pink, $35.

Popular pitcher produced in the 1930s for serving drinks. Green, 8", TITA, $35.

Independence Day, the memorable 4th of July. The colors red, white, and blue played a significant part in this holiday. These colors were displayed in flags all over. **Left to right:** bowl, 6-1/2", nappy, Coronation, "Banded Fine Rib," "Saxon," $12; bowl, 5-3/8", cereal, Aurora, $18; bowl, 6", fruit, Vitrock, "Flower Rim," $6.

DEFINING DEPRESSION GLASS

What amazes me, given the numerous collectors of Depression Glass and the spate of books on this subject, is the number of people who still ask, "What is Depression Glass?" When I mentioned that I had written a book on this subject, that question came up several times. Some could recall the pink and green glassware that their grandmother had, but had only a vague idea of the other beautiful colors: yellow, blue, red, white, amethyst, and yellow.

Depression Glass still needs some definition. It is the colored glassware that made its advent in the late 1920s and was produced totally by the machine method. As we have noted, this was the era of the Great Depression—the severe financial period that gripped America. The glassware derived its name from this turbulent era. Out of these years came the hundreds of pieces of this colored and transparent machine made glassware.

This glassware has definite characteristics that result from the method in which it was produced: the tank molding process. The ingredients of mixed silica, soda ash, limestone, and sand were first heated in a ceramic tank. The liquid glass, along with coloring agents, was then forced through pipes into an automated pressing mold. The glassware took on the shape of the mold in various decorations in relief from the designs or patterns tooled in the mold.

Different mold methods—mold etched, pressed, chipped, cut, or paste—provided the variations in this inexpensive glassware. Much of the collectible glassware was decorated by the *mold etched* pattern process. This method was a unique and clever way of imitating the more expensive technique of plate etching glassware. The pattern was cut in the mold and then became a raised design in relief etching. This was a particularly successful aspect of depression glass design. Many of the designs were placed on the outside of the glassware for practical purposes, such as not collecting the food. In the *pressed* mold method, the glassware was pressed out of a shaped mold, requiring less craftsmanship in the preparation than the etched. The *chipped* method involved the cutting of the pattern by a tool procedure. Intricate and flat patterns could be achieved by this means, but the etched appearance would not be present and the designs would be less complex than with the popular etched mold process. The *cut* mold method, an older method, was used to simulate the many faceted appearance of cut glass. This is a deeply cut type of mold design and an intricate pattern. Finally, the *paste* mold method involved keeping the iron molds at a continually high temperature throughout the molding process and then intermittently cooling them. There were few mold marks but it was a more expensive method. These methods by which the molds were decorated produced the inexpensive glassware sold during the Depression Era, an interesting and informative factor for all collectors and non collectors to know.

What also amazes me is how the glass designers were so creative and innovative in the 1920s and 1930s. A glass mold was a costly thing to make and most of the patterns in Depression Glass we find today must have been carefully designed for production.

Color was strongly emphasized. The use of the coloring agents had a strong impact on the popularity of this glassware both then and today. Similarly, the shapes and various designs appealed to the '20s generation and appeal to the '90s generation, too.

It is significant to know that this popular glassware had a definite purpose adapting to the eating habits and needs of that particular time. Various bowls of different sizes were used for serving cereals, sauces, and desserts. All types of plates—bread and butter, luncheon, dinner, dessert, salad, cake, grill, and torte or chop—were used for meal purposes and in restaurants. Pitchers, creamers, sugars, and butter dishes completed the dinnerware sets.

Back in that era, meals were the highlight of the day and the table settings were completely coordinated in the various sizes and colors. All of the glassware produced was used daily for serving meals.

Most veteran collectors want to know the exact description of this glassware and the name "Depression Glass." To summarize, therefore, Depression Glass is the machine made, mass produced, colored, transparent, inexpensive glass produced in the 1920s and 1930s, the turbulent years known as the Great Depression.

Cut Mold, Floral and Diamond Band, U.S. Glass Co., late 1920s. This is a sharply cut and well designed pattern reminiscent of cut glass. Very attractive in the floral and diamond design. Sugar, 5-1/4", $15; sugar lid, $65; creamer, 4-3/4", $20.

Mold Etched Plate, No. 612, "Horseshoe," Indiana Glass Co., 1930-1933. This pattern shows an interesting use of the mold etched technique for glass decoration. The entire plate surface is one uninterrupted design. The elaborate design of scroll work, undecorated, forms a snowflake pattern. A coveted pattern. Plate, 9-3/8", luncheon, green, $14.

Mold Etched Creamer and Sugar, No. 612, "Horseshoe," Indiana Glass Co., 1930-1933. Creamer, ftd., $19; sugar, ftd., open, $17, yellow.

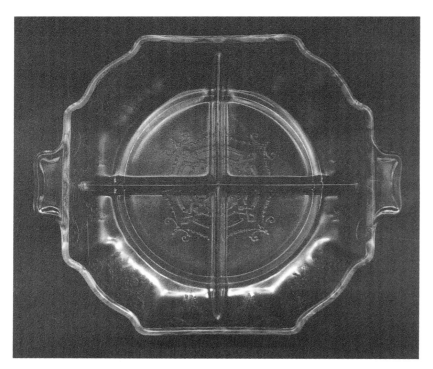

Mold Etched Plate, Lorain "Basket," No. 615, Indiana Glass Co., 1929-1932. This pattern is attractive, with conventional baskets of flowers in more contemporary shapes than most mold etched glass. Very striking with the center motifs of scrolls and garlands surrounded by an eight sided swag ending in finials and scrolls. It's rather a scarce search for these pieces. Pale yellow is more abundant. Plate, 8", relish, 4 part, crystal, $16.

Mold Etched Plate, Lorain, "Basket," No. 615, Indiana Glass Co., 1929-1932. Plate, 8-3/8", luncheon, crystal, $18.

Mold Etched Platter, Lorain, "Basket," No. 615, Indiana Glass Co., 1929-1932. Platter, 11-1/2", oval, yellow, $45.

Paste Mold, Heritage, Federal Glass Co., 1940-1955. Bowl, 10-1/2", fruit, $15.

Paste Mold, Heritage, Federal Glass Co., 1940-1955. This is a later pattern but popular, and fashioned to resemble traditional old Sandwich Glass designs. An extremely attractive pattern in crystal with a flower design in a petal and beaded effect. Plate, 12", sandwich, $15.

Paste Mold, Heritage, Federal Glass Co., 1940-1955. **Left to right:** bowl, 5", berry, $8; bowl, 8-1/2", large berry, $40; bowl, 5", berry, $8.

Pressed Mold Place Setting, Diana, Federal Glass Co., 1937-1941. This is a simple pattern of fine swirled radial lines leading out from the center of the plates and wide rims of slightly larger radial curved lines. This pressed mold pattern was produced for about four years. **Left to right:** bowl, 5", cereal, $10; bowl, 9", salad, $20; bowl, 5", cereal, $10, pink.

Set, Bowl and Plate, Diana, Federal Glass Co., 1937-1941. Plate, 11-3/4", sandwich, $10; bowl, 11", console, fruit, $20, amber.

Place Setting, Diana, Federal Glass Co., 1937-1941. Plate, 9-1/2", dinner, $9; cup, $7; saucer, $2, amber.

Place Setting, Diana, Federal Glass Co., 1937-1941. Plate, 11-3/4", sandwich, with band of gold trim, $10; cup, $3; saucer, $2, crystal.

Chipped Mold, Sharon, "Cabbage Rose," Federal Glass Co., 1935-1939. This is the popular pattern that was owned by most everyone, at least a piece, back in the 1930s. It was best remembered as the basic dinnerware set. The off-center motif of a curved spray of roses with spokes makes it so attractive. **Left to right:** bowl, 5", berry, $9; cup, $9; plate, 9-1/2", dinner, $12, amber.

Set, Sharon, "Cabbage Rose," Federal Glass Co., 1935-1939. **Left to right:** sugar, ftd., $9; creamer, ftd., $14, amber.

Bowl, Sharon, "Cabbage Rose," Federal Glass Co., 1935-1939. 8-1/2", berry, amber, $6.

Bowl, Sharon, "Cabbage Rose," Federal Glass Co., 1935-1939. 10-1/2", fruit, amber, $23.

Chipped Mold, Rosemary, "Dutch Rose," Federal Glass Co., 1935-1937. An attractive and conservative pattern that appeals to those collectors who do not like the busier chipped mold design. The dinner plate has a center bouquet of full blown roses and a rim of roses placed between overlapping designs. Plate, dinner, $9; cup, $6; saucer, $4.

Chipped Mold, Rosemary, "Dutch Rose," Federal Glass Co., 1935-1937. **Left to right:** creamer, $9; plate, 6-3/4", salad, $6; sugar, $9.

Cut Mold, Cube, "Cubist," Jeannette Glass Co., 1929-1933. A pattern in name and in shape very contemporary, reflecting what was going on in the world of fine arts at that particular time. Consists of diamond cut crystal deeply indented blocks. This is an "eye catching" design which attracts new collectors. Collectors often confuse this pattern with Fostoria's American. There is a discernible difference; the color is the main factor with a clearer and more brilliant look in American. Cube is not as heavy. Tray for sugar and creamer with gold trim, 7-1/2", $5; sugar, 2-3/8", $2; creamer, 2-5/8", $2.

Cut Mold, Cube, "Cubist," Jeannette Glass Co., 1929-1933. Bowl, 4-1/2", deep, plain, $3; crystal bowl, 4-1/2", deep with gold trim, $4.

Opposite page, bottom:
Place Setting, Cube, "Cubist," Jeannette Glass Co., 1929-1933. **Left to right:** sherbet, ftd., $8; plate, 8", luncheon, $7; cup, $9; saucer, $3, green.

Cut Mold, Cube, "Cubist," Jeannette Glass Co., 1929-1933. **Left to right:** creamer, 2-5/8", $3; plate, 8", luncheon, $7; sugar, 2-3/8", $3.

Paste Mold, Columbia, Federal Glass Co., 1938-1942. This is a later pattern made in two colors, pink and crystal. Pink is difficult to find. This has a bull's eye design in the center surrounded by a sunburst with large beading inside the rim. The outer rim is decorated with radial rows of graduated circles. Plate, 9-1/2", luncheon, $10; cup, $9; saucer, $3.

Accessories, Paste Mold, Columbia, Federal Glass Co., 1938-1942. Plate, 11", chop, $12; bowl, 10-1/2", ruffled edge, $20.

How Did This Glassware
Gain Such Popularity?

Collectors are still searching harder than ever for the colored glassware known as Depression Glass. All of this beautiful glassware, sometimes labeled the All American Collectible, overwhelms the collectors from the 1920s to the 1930s. Rich in history, this glassware has become a very significant part of the culture from this period. Depression Glass as a collectible has grown so rapidly that the enormous number of collectors is phenomenal. The glamour of the glassware as described in 1929, when it was sold to serve food, is glamorized today in its search, display, enjoyment, and preservation. Throughout our travels, it is just amazing to see the amount of collectors hunting and browsing through antique shops and flea markets to match pieces for their sets, for investment purposes, or for the sheer beauty and the challenge. Maybe they are searching for that rare piece or the "sleeper." Many remark how glad they were that they had stopped at this shop, thereby finding their "goodies."

A Manhattan vase by Manhattan, Anchor Hocking Glass Co., 1932-1939. A very popular pattern with the sharp rib appearance, inherited by many household members. 8", $18.

Bowl, Adam, by Jeannette Glass Co., 1932-1934. A common inherited piece of this delicate looking pattern with a center group of alternating feathers and plumes accented with wide radial ridges and rims. 7-3/4", $28.

With such an intense interest in collecting this glassware, one wonders just what is behind all this. Sometimes I think it's just plain old fashioned nostalgia, bringing back the fond memories from the years in which it was produced. Many recall these years as "the good old days." It never fails to amaze me that the generation of today would be so interested in this so-called "old glass." This is actually true because I inherited my first piece from my grandmother and I know that is how so many collectors got started.

Shopping or just browsing for this glassware is a great way to pass the time away, not only on vacation but on your days off from work or just in some spare hours. So many of my collector friends engage in this activity. Also, vacationing guests enjoy visiting the various shops in different areas.

Younger people have developed a keener appreciation for this glassware, as we see more and more visiting the antique stores. With the dinnerware given away at the local grocery stores and movies in the '20s and '30s becoming such a hot collectible, collectors are on the search for it. This glass dinnerware, in fanciful designs etched in the molds by automatic methods that produced such lovely settings, is certainly worth the hunt.

There is a striking similarity between the families in the 1920s and 1930s and the collectors of today. The 1920s and '30s housewives were scouting around picking up pieces for a dime or less to complete sets for the family table. Today, we collectors are doing the same thing trying to assemble our sets. However, we are not as fortunate at finding the pieces so cheap.

The treasure hunting goes on, hoping the "sleeper" or the good "find" will be discovered. Sometimes we are lucky even when we are not looking for anything. With the ongoing great passion for this colored glassware, many of us wish in retrospect that we had saved some of these pieces!

Bowl, Miss America, by Anchor Hocking Glass Co., 1935-1938. This pattern, with the hobnail motif and large sunburst of radial lines, is highly collectible. A cherished piece inherited from my grandmother. 8", curved in at the top, $75.

Grill plate, Daisy, "620," Indiana Glass Co., late 1930s. An early pattern in crystal with the design of daisies around the border for its characteristic motif. Widely used in restaurants. 10-3/8", $6.

Goblets, Mayfair, "Open Rose," by Anchor Hocking Glass Co., 1931-1937. One of the "star" patterns so widely used and attractive with the center circle of roses and widely spaced lines. My favorite inherited goblet. 5-3/4", 9 oz., water, $70 each.

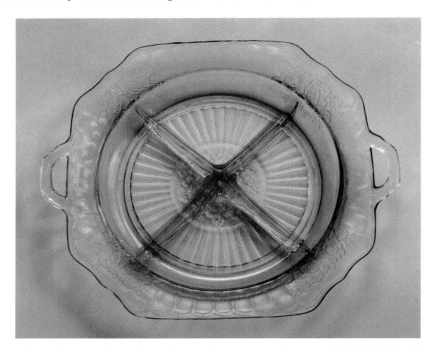

Relish Plate, Mayfair, "Open Rose," by Anchor Hocking Glass Co., 1931-1937. 8- 3/4", 4 part, $33.

Bowl, Cherry Blossom, Jeannette Glass Co., 1930-1939. A favorite of so many collectors with the captivating, all over pattern of profuse cherry blossoms divided by distinct panels. A true Depression pattern in an opaque glass color. Still very popular among collectors in spite of the reproductions. 9", 2 handled, $45.

Bowl by Duncan and Miller, 1926-1930s, called a console, reversible, very unique and popular back in that era. Found when shopping for the unusual, browsing through the antique shops. 14" flower or Gardenia Ring, rose-pink, $50-$60.

Vase, Ring, "Banded Rings," 1927-1933. An early pattern in Depression Glass with the horizontal ribbed bands in a circle pattern. 8", iridescent, $15, uncommon.

Candy Dish and Cover, Queen Mary (Prismatic Line), vertical ribbed, Anchor Hocking Glass Co., 1936-1949. This pattern is becoming more popular, with the vertical ribs and sunburst of radiating lines surrounded by a circular band. This brilliant candy dish was a long search for my collection. $22.

Place Setting, "Bubble," "Bullseye," "Provincial," Anchor Hocking Glass Co., 1934-1965. This is an easy pattern for young collectors to identify, with the scalloped edges and the centers with a radial sunburst ending in a circle of bull's eye dots. Crystal is quite common and affordable. Plate, 9-3/8", dinner, $6; tumbler, 9 oz., water, $6; cup, $3; saucer, $1.

Place Setting, Block Optic, "Block," Anchor Hocking Glass Co., 1929-1933. This pattern has always attracted new collectors due to its availability. The design has a typical 1930s look about it with wide concentric circles set off in blocks. It has a heavy appearance but is rather fragile for machine made glassware. Plate, 9", dinner, $25; cup, $7; saucer, $10.

Place Setting, Diamond Quilted, "Flat Diamond," Imperial Glass Co., late 1920s to early 1930s. A simple pressed pattern in a quilted diamond effect. Center of plates is plain and borders consist of a diamond design. Ideal as a luncheon set for young collectors. Sherbet, $5; plate, 8", luncheon, $6; cup, $9.

Sugar and Creamer, Diamond Quilted, "Flat Diamond," $8 each.

Accessories, Diamond Quilted, "Flat Diamond". Candlestick, $13; bowl, 5", $8; candlestick, $13.

Place Setting, "S" Pattern, "Stippled Rose Band," MacBeth-Evans Glass Co., 1930-1933. This is a popular set to use for its delicate lacy pattern. It has a circular motif in the center, surrounded by an arrangement of leaves and fine stippling. The outer rim has a band of the leaf motifs and stippling edged by groups of three leaves and scrolled designs. These scrolls give the pattern its name. Plate, 8", luncheon, $5; tumbler, 4-3/4", 10 oz., $7; saucer, $2; cup, $4.

Accessories, "S" Pattern, "Stippled Rose Band." Sugar, $6; bowl, 5-1/2", cereal, $5; creamer, $6.

Basic pieces, "S" Pattern, "Stippled Rose Band." Plate, 9-1/4", dinner, amber, $9; cup, $5.

Basic piece, "S" Pattern, "Stippled Rose Band." Plate, 9-1/4", dinner, amber, $9.

Candleholders. Depression candleholders in the typical color, green, used with a console bowl as a centerpiece or for other decorative purposes. 3", $20 pr.

PROMOTIONAL GIVEAWAY PREMIUMS

There is renewed interest in the Depression Glass given away at the grocery stores, hardware stores, and variety stores with purchases of packaged items, dairy products, furniture, refrigerators, seeds, and gasoline. Right now it's becoming more popular and will continue to be a hot collectible in the near future.

Since I mentioned the "giveaways" at the various sources listed above in my first book, the interest in these premiums has been incredible. I've talked with so many of the older generation (senior citizens) who vividly recall these premium gifts. They looked forward to these beautiful and varied pieces of glassware with eager anticipation and they were anxious to share their information with me.

Premium gifts helped to increase additions to the sets of dinnerware that the housewives were trying to assemble in the 1920s and 1930s. This was a great incentive for making purchases and very beneficial for the business merchants. The customers were very happy and the business people very pleased as well.

The giveaway premiums promoting the sale of such products played a very significant role in the popularity of this highly collectible glassware. Much of the Depression Glass was distributed through the familiar variety stores for as little as three to four cents. Imagine that! This was a very welcome purchase for the people living in that era. Black glassware, now becoming one of my favorites, was one of the abundant pieces available.

The promotional items or premiums were produced primarily by Federal, Hazel Atlas, and Anchor Hocking Companies. Sears and Roebuck offered its customers a complete set of dinnerware for $1.99. What a bargain! Anything was welcomed in this period. Businesses would stress to their customers, "Glass is right and glamorous."

I was deeply saddened by the closing of the Woolworth and Kresge dime stores, as so much of this beautiful glassware was sold throughout these stores. Cherished memories will always remain in the hearts of the people buying this glassware.

All of this glassware earned its way into the collectible field of American Glassware.

Premiums, Ring, "Banded Rings," Anchor Hocking Glass Co., 1927-1932. An earlier pattern in Depression Glass that resembles a modern look with the horizontal ribbed bands and circle pattern in various colored bands and solid colors. In the color pink, the pitcher and tumblers were dairy premiums. Green could also have been one. **Left to right:** pitcher, 8-1/2", 80 oz., pink, ice lip, $35; pitcher, 8-1/2", 80 oz., green, plain lip, $35.

Premiums, Tumblers, 4-3/4", 10 oz., pink, $10 each. These tumblers originally contained cottage cheese.

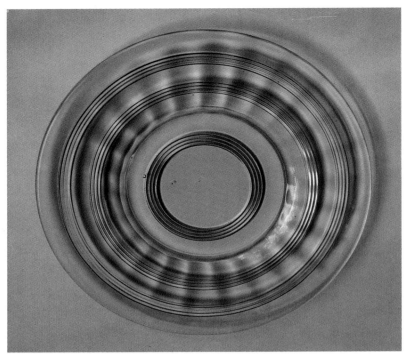

Premium, Plate, 11-1/4", sandwich, green, $14.

Premium, Pitcher, cobalt blue with the photographic image of Shirley Temple. 4-1/2", $48. A high milk pitcher from the breakfast set.

Premium, Creamer, "Aurora," Hazel Atlas Glass Co., late 1930s. This cobalt blue creamer was a premium gift given away for buying a breakfast cereal. What a beautiful gift to receive. 4-1/2", $25.

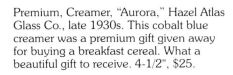

Premiums. These pieces were given away as premiums for buying Wheaties and Bisquick. This breakfast set consisted of the bowl, mug, and pitcher with the photographic image of this popular child actress. Highly cherished among collectors. **Top row left to right:** pitcher, $48; mug, $50. **Center:** bowl, $60.

Premiums. Black glassware items were premium gifts. L.E. Smith Glass Co., 1920-1934, produced black glassware in abundance that was sold at hardware stores in the Midwestern states. Many pieces were promoted as premiums. Mt. Pleasant "Double Shield," bonbon, 7", rolled-up handles, $23; bowl, 6", two-handled, square, $18.

Premium, Place Setting, Petalware, MacBeth-Evans Glass Co., 1930-1940. This pattern, with versatile designs of floral motifs, colored bands, and concentric circles, was a premium by a milling company. The product was Roseware Oats, found in the West as the mills were located in Seattle, San Francisco, Portland, and Los Angeles. Each three pound box of Alber's Oats contained a piece of Petalware: a cup, saucer, plates, cereal bowl, and a sherbet. Plate, 9", dinner, $9; plate, 8", salad, $5; cup, $5; saucer, $2.

Premium, Sherbet, Roxana by Hazel Atlas Glass Co., 1932. This pattern has a unique, four pointed design emanating in the form of a cross. The same motif with three leaf-like designs adorns the border along alternate sides. In the package of "Star Brand Oats" a piece of "Golden Topaz," or Roxana as we know it today, was found. Sherbet, ftd., $12.

Premiums, Refrigerator Sets. With the purchase of a refrigerator, customers received special refrigerator sets for storing food as premium gifts. These were very practical gifts. **Left to right:** butter dish, crisscross, $20; storage box with cover, 4" x 8", embossed with fruit motifs, $19; food saver, $8.

Plate, Normandie, "Bouquet and Lattice," Federal Glass Co., 1933-1940. This pattern has a beautiful, wrought mold etched floral all over design. Interestingly, this glassware was shipped to the Great Northern Products Company in train carloads to be used as premiums. Plate, 11", dinner, $33, scarce.

Premiums, Hobnail, Hocking Glass Co., 1934-1936. This is an adaptation of a traditional glass pattern. Originally it was made in both crystal and pink. Centers of plates consist of radial lines in a sunburst effect. Rims have raised dots or hobnails. Pink hobnail, the color "Rose Glass" pink, was made especially in 1935 for premiums consisting of sherbets, 8-1/2" plate, 6" saucer or sherbet plate, and the cup. **Left to right:** cup, $5; saucer, $2; sherbet, $5.

Sherbet, Manhattan, "Horizontal Ribbed," Anchor Hocking Glass Co., 1938-1943. Some pieces in this pattern with metal attachments were produced in other factories. Hocking sold some of these items to other companies who added these attachments to them. This could be one of them, a special promotional item. Sherbet in a metal holder with fork, $15.

Place Setting, American Sweetheart, by MacBeth-Evans Glass Co., 1930-1936. One of the most popular of any of their patterns, with a neat arrangement of a center motif of festoons, ribbons, and scroll designs plus smaller ones surrounding the scalloped rim. Has ten short radial lines to the border. Pink and white were given away with the purchase of vegetable and flower seeds by the American Seed Company. Plate, 9-3/4" to 10-1/4", dinner, $26; cup, $11; saucer, $2, monax.

Place Setting, pink, American Sweetheart. Plate, 9-3/4" to 10-1/4", dinner, $39; cup, $20; saucer, $4.

Premium, Plate, "Bubble," "Bullseye," "Provincial," Anchor Hocking Glass Co., 1929-1933. This plate, 9-3/8" dinner, is 1/8" larger than the normally found dinner plate. The center of the plate is smaller, with four rows of bubbles outside the center. The normally found dinner plate has three rings of bubbles that are smaller and hard to find. This larger plate is a premium item that was found in a bag of flour. Plate, 9-3/8", dinner, $8.

Premium, Tray with Sugar and Creamer, Sandwich, Indiana Glass Co., 1920s. An attractive pattern with the all over stippling spaced around flower, foliage, and scroll motifs in an elaborate arrangement. A traditional pattern in pressed glass. Sugar and creamer on the tray was a premium gift given away with "Big Joe," a 100 pound sack of flour at a grocery store. Tray, diamond-shaped, $3; creamer, $9; sugar, $9.

THE CAPTIVATING COLORS

In the production of Depression Glass, the various colors were strongly emphasized. The use of the coloring agents had a strong impact on the popularity of the glassware both then and today.

Cobalt blue is an extremely popular color among collectors. Its origin started with the advertising items, such as ash trays, mugs, pitchers, and bowls. We are all familiar with the breakfast set, the mug, pitcher, and cereal bowl featuring the photographic image of Shirley Temple as a premium gift for purchasing cereal in the boxes. Wouldn't this entice anyone to purchase an item in this color? The romantic history of this color is interesting. Back in my teens, there was this one perfume called "Evening In Paris" which came in a cobalt blue vial with the tassel on top. It was my favorite and my mother would buy it for me quite often. I had quite a collection displayed in my room and I was fascinated in the way it was labeled, "A Romance Colored Cobalt Blue." What a memory! Cobalt blue glassware produced by several glass companies is regarded by some as the most familiar of any Depression Glass item. Collecting some of these pieces has started me on the journey of trying to acquire more of this vintage. This is a scarce color, perhaps a "sleeper" in many of the patterns. Collectors have to search for this color, a strong rich blue with a mystique all of its own.

Amethyst, a light pastel purple, is equally as popular as cobalt blue. This rich purplish color is also scarce in many of the patterns. Some of the companies called this purplish color burgundy. It was interesting to learn that this color was made by the addition of nickel or manganese. This color is a favorite of my husband and many of my collector friends.

Black, the striking, elegant, and rich color, has recently captured my admiration. In my years of collecting, I have seen so little of it and it was always quite expensive. All of a sudden this glassware is surfacing more and more in the Midwest, especially in the antique stores. One dealer had such a large quantity of it that she wanted to gradually decrease her collection. I lucked out and acquired some very pretty pieces. My collection is mainly for decorative purposes, intermixed with crystal and other colors. The prices of this glassware seem more moderate.

Some of the black glassware was a promotional item in the hardware stores of the early '30s. It surprised me that this type of glass was a premium gift. Not only is this glassware striking, it is also very durable. To "prove" its durability, I accidentally fell and knocked over a shelf with several pieces of my newly acquired glassware and not one piece was broken!

Cobalt Blue, a very rich and popular color that was produced widely by several companies in the 1920s and 1930s. Many advertising pieces were produced in this color. "Aurora," Hazel Atlas Co., late 1920s. This is a limited pattern and is no longer cheap to collect. Shocking to me was the price of the 4-1/2" deep bowl, $55. I cherish every piece with the bands at the top and the closely knit ribs in this small set. **Left to right:** bowl, 4-1/2", deep, $55; creamer, 4-1/2", $25; cup, $15; plate, 6-1/2", $12; bowl, 5-3/8", $18; tumbler, 4-3/4", 10 oz., $25.

Various pieces of this popular color. **Clockwise from left:** vase, $10; vase, etched bud, $18; vase, ruffled top, $22; figurine, fish, $10.

Amethyst, a purple or violet color is admired by collectors and is extremely popular. Moderntone, Hazel Atlas Glass Co., 1934-1942, late 1940s to early 1950s. A pressed pattern that typifies the decorative art style of the 1930s. Very innovative for the time, containing widely spaced concentric rings with a modern look. **Left to right:** cream soup, 5", $34; plate, 5-7/8", $5; plate, 8-3/8", dinner, $14; cup, $11; saucer, $4.

Variety of vases in amethyst. **Left to right:** vase, $22; vase, $10; vase, bud, etched, $18.

Moroccan, Amethyst, Hazel Ware, Division of Continental Can, 1960s. A pleasing purplish color of the various moulds of Hazel Ware glass. Popular in the square, rectangular, octagonal, and swirled shapes. **Left to right:** bowl, 6", round, $11; bowl, 9-3/4", rectangular, with metal handle, $18; bowl, 6", round, $11.

Newport, "Hairpin," Hazel Atlas Glass Co., 1936-1940. An attractive pattern called "Hairpin" by some collectors. It has overlapping hairpin lines on the borders. A very beautiful amethyst color. Plate, 8-13/16", dinner, $30.

Serving pieces in amethyst. **Left to right:** creamer with crystal handle, $8; bowl with pouring spout, $10.

The L.E. Smith Company will be best remembered for the production of black glass originating in the 1920s and was the biggest producer of black glass. The pattern, Mt. Pleasant, "Double Shield," is easy to recognize with scalloped edges and alternating one and two points.

Black was Diamond's foremost color and many specialties were produced in gold and silver encrustations and trims. Their console sets are something to admire. U.S. Glass produced the black glassware with beautiful, decorated etchings and a satin finish.

Black Amethyst. This glass appears black until it is held to the light, then a dark purple can be seen. This was made in many factories from 1860 to the 1900s, much in the 1930s. Vase, 7-1/2", black amethyst, $65.

Van Deman produced the very popular "Black Forest," deeply etched and embellished with white gold encrustations.

Imperial's glass is recognized by its etched or cut colored lines with gold bands.

New Martinsville and Westmoreland produced the black glassware in combination with jade, crystal, and topaz in 1929 and 1930.

Hazel Atlas became popular with Floral Sterling luncheon sets, signed sterling on flowerleaf.

Morganton was known for its numerous bridge sets and beverage sets in black and crystal.

Lotus was famous for its black glassware with a banding of 24 kt. gold. Their assortment of console sets, sandwich trays, fruit bowls, salad sets, pitchers, and goblets in sterling silver are absolutely exquisite.

Fenton produced black or ebony glass for a great part of its history. Ebony glassware was also made by Duncan and Miller, and their color—the striking jet black—stands out with its superb brilliancy.

Other companies produced brilliant console sets, handled bonbons, card trays, sugar and creamer sets on trays, elegant vases, dresser sets, and cake and sandwich trays.

Little did I realize how elegant this glassware is and what a variety of items were made until I did some extensive researching and checking of what I could find at the antique stores. Searching for this is now my challenge.

Pieces in black amethyst. Swan, $20; bowl, 3 ftd., $22.

Mt. Pleasant "Double Shield," by L.E. Smith Glass Co., 1920s to 1934. This pattern in black has scalloped edges with alternating one and two points, making it easy to identify. This is striking and quality glassware. Bowl, mayonnaise, 5-1/2", 3 ftd., $30; plate, 7", 2 handled, scalloped, $15.

Mt. Pleasant "Double Shield" sandwich server, center handled, $40.

Black glassware painted with designs of flowers and fruits in red, green, yellow, blue, and white was popular in the 1930s. L.E. Smith and U.S. Glass Companies promoted this quite highly. Some other companies that produced black glass promoted it too, with silver bands and other decorations. **Left to right:** bowl, 6", handled, square, $20; vase, 9-3/4", with crimped top and two red bands, $15; vase, 6", 2 handled with gold trim, $22; compote with decorated top, $22.

Vase, 8", crimped top in black, 2 handled, with sterling floral design, $45.

Black decorated cookie jar (without lid), $25.

Black compote, 6-1/4", square with beveled corners and points at intervals, $35.

Black, Ovide, Hazel Atlas Glass Co., 1930-1935. **Left to right:** creamer, $7; saucer, $4; cup, $7; sugar, $7.

Black with sterling floral decoration. Sugar, $9; creamer, $9.

Black, Ovide, Hazel Atlas Glass Co., 1930-1935. Candy dish and cover, $45; stand, $15.

Crystal on black. Cup, Starlight, $5; saucer, $7; cup, Waterford "Waffle," $6; saucer, $7. An attractive combination.

Crystal on black. Bowl, 8", scalloped, Sandwich, $8; on stand, $15; bowl, 6-1/2", scalloped, Sandwich, $7; on stand, $9.

Candlesticks, Mt. Pleasant "Double Shield," $30 pr.; bowl, 9-3/8", Pretzel, $18. A beautiful centerpiece.

Topaz, the rich, soft, bright yellow, is not seen too often in this area, the midwestern United States. This color is more of an elegant color and much of it is found in the Lancaster elegant glassware line. The companies producing this color were Cambridge, Fostoria, Imperial, and some by Fenton, Anchor Hocking, and Hazel Atlas. This glassware was produced in the late 1920s and 1930s. The name Topaz was changed to Gold Tin and Golden Glow by some of the companies.

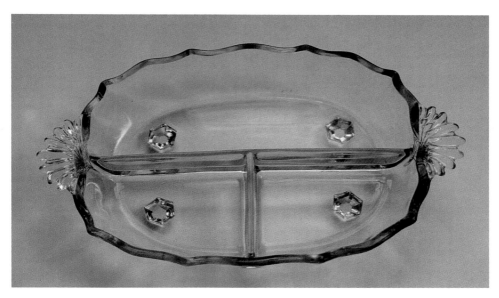

Topaz, a soft yellow color produced mainly in the elegant glassware that has become a collector's dream. Bowl, Baroque Line, #2496, Fostoria Glass Co., 1936-1966, 10", relish, 3 part, scalloped edge, $23.

Topaz, Baroque Line, #2496, by Fostoria. Bowl, 4", handled, ftd., $20; bowl, 6-1/2", 2 part, $20.

Pink, the soft, yet brilliant *eye* catching color, is always associated with Depression Glass. It is one of the classic colors recognized by the majority of collectors and non-collectors. It is sometimes called "grandma's glass." The majority of the popular glass companies produced this color.

Pink, the eye-catching and classic color in Depression Glass that appeals to all collectors. Sunflower, Jeannette Glass Co., late 1920s. This pattern has a stylized sunflower enclosed by plain undecorated glass. Border contains large flowers and foliage. **Left to right:** tumbler, 4-3/4", 8 oz., ftd., $28; plate, 9", dinner, $17; saucer, $8; cup, $12.

Opposite page, bottom:
Green, New Century and incorrectly, "Lydia Ray," Hazel Atlas Glass Co., 1930-1935. This was a previously unidentified pattern. Contains a small bull's eye center with widely spaced vertical lines leading to the border in a sunburst effect. Border consists of vertical lines. Plate, 10", dinner, $20.

Green, the vibrant and refreshing color, attracts collectors and non-collectors alike. Like pink, it is the classic color associated with Depression Glass and can also be labeled "grandma's glass." There are many variations of color in green and it was given different names by different companies. I grew up with a lot of this green colored glassware along with the pink.

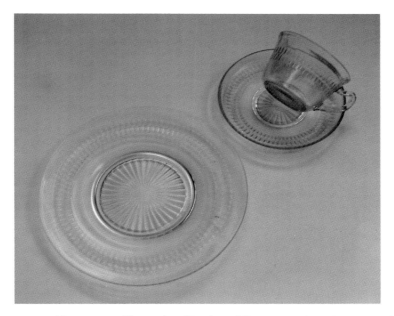

Green is a typical Depression Glass color. "Roulette," "Many Windows," Hocking Glass Co., 1935-1939. This is another pressed pattern, very plain in appearance. Center has an outburst of radial lines and border consists of block shapes in center of rim. Plate, 8-1/2", luncheon, $6; cup, $7; saucer, $4.

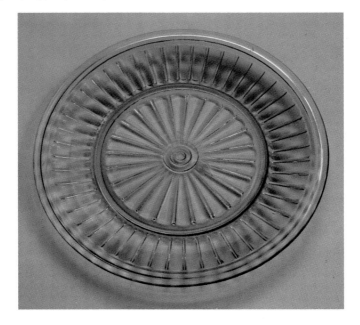

Amber, a darkish yellow, was produced by some of the major glass companies, such as Indiana, Federal, MacBeth, Jeannette, and McKee. The color is gaining in popularity and is growing on me since I started to collect the pattern, "Daisy."

Amber, a darkish yellow color, is gaining in popularity. Daisy, No. 620, 1933, 1940-1960. An attractive pattern with the prominent daisy design. Plate, 9-3/8", dinner, $9; tumbler, 9 oz., ftd., $18; saucer, $2; cup, $6.

Amber, Normandie, "Bouquet and Lattice." Plate, 11", $33.

Amber, Normandie, "Bouquet and Lattice," Federal Glass Co., 1933-1940. This pattern has a beautiful, delicate all over wrought mold etched design. Creamer, $9; sugar, $8.

Amber, Sandwich, Indiana Glass Co., 1920-1970s. Bowl, 8-1/2", $11.

Yellow, a primary classic color, was produced by many of the glass companies. Like a lemon, this color took on different shades—greenish, golden and orangish. Many of the yellow pieces were decorated in various designs. Floral was popular.

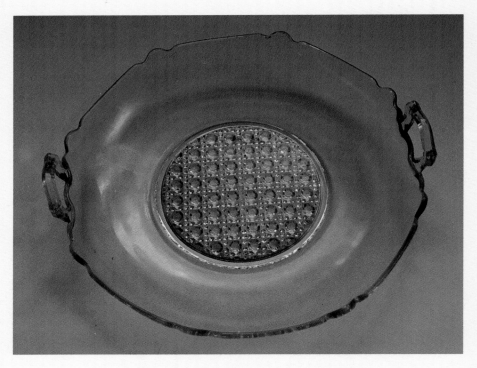

Elegant Glassware. Much beautiful glassware was produced in the yellow color. Lancaster Glass Co., 1930s. Bowl, with handles for serving, $25.

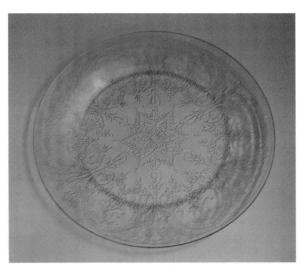

Yellow, a primary classic color which takes on different shades and was produced in unique designs, No. 612, "Horseshoe," Indiana Glass Co., 1930-1933. This pattern has an elaborate design of scroll work, undecorated, which forms a snowflake pattern. Plate, 9-3/8", luncheon, $15.

Elegant Glassware. Bowl, uniquely designed, $35.

Ultra-marine, a blue-green color, is admired by nearly everyone. This color is scarce and some think it is rare. The Jeannette Glass Company was the main producer of this color. It was the big hit of 1937 and 1938.

Ultramarine, a very admired blue-green color but quite scarce. "Swirl," "Petal Swirl," Jeannette Glass Co., 1937-1938. An attractive pattern with a motif of concentric ribbed circles and an outer rim of swirled ribs in the border. Sugar, $16; bowl, 5-1/4", cereal, $18; creamer, $16.

Iridescent was produced by applying an iridized spray over crystal pieces and then reheating. Sometime the pieces look like a rainbow of colors with a brilliant shine. On the pieces I have, there is a strong iridized color. On some, however, there can be a weak color. Observe the colors on the glassware you purchase carefully. Many collectors are attracted to this color.

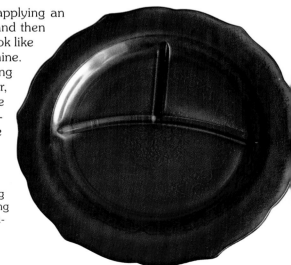

Iridescent, a color produced by applying an iridized spray on crystal pieces, giving it a shine. Plate, grill, Normandie, "Bouquet and Lattice," $9.

Crystal is actually clear glass. Many think that Depression Glass was just colored. This is not true, as many of the popular patterns were produced in crystal. There are so many attractive and versatile serving pieces in crystal.

Crystal, clear glass produced in many patterns. "Daisy," No. 620, Indiana Glass Co., 1933. Place setting: plate, 9-3/8", dinner, $6; tumbler, 9 oz., ftd., $10; cup, $4; saucer, $2.

Crystal, Royal Lace candlestick, rolled edge, $30.

Crystal, "Daisy," No. 620. Creamer, $6; sugar, $6.

Crystal, Royal Lace, Hazel Atlas Glass Co., 1934-1941. An outstanding mold etched pattern, very decorative and elaborate with a motif of lacy scrolls, leaves, and flowers surrounded by a drape design. Cup, $7; saucer, $5.

Crystal, Royal Lace plate, 9-7/8", dinner, $16; cup, $7; saucer, $5.

Crystal, Royal Lace plate, 6", sherbet, $5; candlestick, $30; plate, 6", sherbet, $5.

POPULAR PATTERNS
OF THE '20S AND '30S

MANHATTAN, "HORIZONTAL RIBBED"

The Anchor Hocking Glass Company, 1938-1943
Colors: crystal, pink, some green, ruby, and iridized

This pattern has the appearance of one designed to be the "last word" in the '30s. It is in contrast to Hocking's more traditional shapes and patterns. The shape consists of a horizontally wide, sharp ribbed style. It seems as if everyone had some pieces of this in their homes at one time or another. This is a real collector item.

It is difficult to gather a set of this brilliant pink glassware. Some of the hardest pieces to be found in pink are the dinner plates, cups and saucers, and the 42 oz. pitcher. Even some of the basic and extra pieces are scarce. The creamer and sugar and dessert dishes seen to be more available.

Crystal Manhattan seems to be more prevalent, and was produced in the late '30s. Many do not know that Westmoreland Glass Company made some larger pieces in 1929: a sandwich server and bowls in a pink and green design. The salt and pepper shakers are so unique, very small and square.

Manhattan, "Horizontal Ribbed," Anchor Hocking Glass Co., 1938-1943. This pattern was a real collector's item and still is today. **Left to right:** candy dish, 3 legs, $11; compote, 5-3/4", $35; bowl, 5-3/8", with handles, $18, pink, scarce.

A real find is the compete Lazy Susan relish server with the five inserts. I am very fond of these sets and love to display them, especially with the red inserts.

Interesting are the pieces with the metal attachments that were produced in other factories. The Hocking Company sold some of these to other companies who added the metal attachments to these products. At first I debated about purchasing them but now they add a different touch. They may have been promotional items. I enjoy using the small, 4-1/2" sherbet bowl with the metal holder for mints. Look-alike pieces can be added but many prefer the real pattern.

Cereal bowls and the ash tray are scarce.

The collector should know that some of the items are not true Manhattan, including the covered candy dish, little wines, double candle holder, the water bottles, and other tumblers. These pieces can blend in nicely with this pattern. It all depends upon how perfect a collector you are.

Crystal Manhattan is recognized as the most original design of the Depression Glass period. The silverish look intrigues many collectors.

Manhattan, relish tray with inserts, $55 (tray, 14", crystal, $16; pink tray inserts, $6 each; sherbet in center, $9).

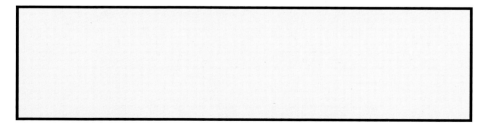

Manhattan. **Left to right:** sugar, $11; tumbler, 10 oz., ftd., $17; creamer, $10, pink, scarce.

Manhattan place setting. **Center:** plate, 10-1/4", dinner, $20. **Left to right:** bowl, 4-1/2", sauce, with handles, $9; tumbler, 10 oz., ftd., $17; cup, $18; saucer, $7.

Manhattan. **Left to right:** creamer, $10; plate, 8-1/2", salad, $15; salt and pepper, 2" square, $28 pr.; sugar, $10.

Manhattan. Bowl, 8", closed handles, $22; bowl, 9-1/2", fruit, $22.

Manhattan. **Left to right:** candlestick, $7.50; bowl, 8", closed handles, $22; candlestick, $7.50.

Manhattan relish tray with inserts in crystal (tray, 14", $16; tray inserts, $5.50 each; sherbet in center, $9;), complete, $53, a find.

Manhattan sherbet in metal attachment, $15.

Manhattan relish tray with inserts (tray, 14", $16; tray inserts in red, $6 each, sherbet in center, $9;), complete, $55.

Manhattan relish tray, 4 part, $18; crystal insert, $9; complete, $27-$30.

Manhattan ash tray with gold trim, $20, scarce.

Manhattan advertising piece. Ash tray with ad, $15-$20, scarce.

Manhattan look-alike, water bottle, $12-$15.

QUEEN MARY (PRISMATIC LINE), "VERTICAL RIBBED"

Hocking Glass Company, 1936-1949
Colors: pink, crystal, and some Royal Ruby

This is a pattern that has received little recognition. To me, it is equally as attractive as Manhattan.

Queen Mary, vertically ribbed with a sunburst of radiating lines surrounded by a circular band, is an attractive pattern, pressed in a brilliant cast. It has a complete table service plus many extras. When this whole set is assembled it is very striking.

The good news is that the crystal is gaining in popularity, and the prices in this pattern are still affordable. This pattern has always appeared to be one of the "sleepers" in crystal.

The challenge in collecting this pattern is finding the pieces in pink. The dinner plates and footed tumblers are extremely difficult to acquire. The prices keep escalating in pink with very little available.

I predict that this pattern in crystal will be very popular among collectors.

Queen Mary (Prismatic Line), vertical ribbed, Hocking Glass Co., 1936-1949. This pattern is gaining in popularity. Vertically ribbed with a sunburst of radiating lines surrounded by a circular band. Striking in a set. Place setting: plate, $18; sherbet, $7; cup, $5; saucer, $2.

Queen Mary. **Left to right:** sugar, $7; plate, 8-1/2", $5; salt and pepper, $22 pr.; creamer, $7.

Queen Mary candlestick, $7.50; compote, $12; candlestick, $7.50.

Queen Mary celery or pickle dish, $12.

Queen Mary plate, 12",
sandwich, $10.

Queen Mary, relish tray, 14", 4
part, $12.

Below:
Queen Mary. **Back row left to
right:** sherbet, ftd., $9; creamer,
$10; cup (small), $11; sugar, $10;
bowl, 4-1/2", berry, $12. **Front
row left to right:** bowl, 4", $5;
bowl, 4", one handle, $5, pink,
scarce.

RING, "BANDED RINGS"

Hocking Glass Company, 1927-1933
Colors: crystal, crystal with pink, red, blue, orange, yellow, black, silver, etc. bands; green, pink, "Mayfair" blue, and Royal Ruby

This pattern is less conventional than other patterns and occurred early in the story of Depression Glass. It is pressed and thin blown. The different green patterns which had the ring design were produced by the Hocking Company. The early motif was called "Circle Design" and produced in 1927. Later on, in 1929, the Ring design was introduced, which had bands of four rings, horizontally ribbed. The pieces of "Circle Design" consisted of four to eight horizontal bands. "Ring" first came in the colors of green and crystal (with platinum rings). Later, it was issued in decorated black, yellow, red, and orange. This is the favorite color that I collect, although I have collected some crystal too.

What intrigues me about this pattern is that it is so complete, especially with the variety of the additional pieces such as the decanter, the cocktail shaker, and the ice bucket. Actually, all of the pieces fascinate me, due to the colors and the fact that they looks so modern today. I use the handled sandwich tray for serving all kinds of snacks almost daily.

The other colors that Ring comes in are crystal with pink, some pink, and "Mayfair" blue and red. These colors are rare.

Even though I live in Wisconsin, I have heard that some collectors have found various pieces in pink, but I have not been fortunate in finding many pieces. I'm enjoying the popular color scheme, black, yellow, red, and orange. A complete set of this pattern is very impressive.

Ring, "Banded Rings," crystal with decoration. Creamer, $6; vase, 8", $35; sugar, $6.

Ring, "Banded Rings," crystal with decoration. **Back row left to right:** sherbet, 4-3/4", ftd., $9; tumbler, 3-1/2", 5 oz., $7; plate, 8", luncheon, $5; plate, 6-1/4", sherbet, $3. **Center left to right:** sherbet, low for 6-1/2" plate, $15; plate, 6-1/2", off-center, $6; cup, $6; saucer, $2.

Ring, "Banded Rings," Hocking Glass Co., 1927-1933. This is an early pressed and thin blown pattern. Very unusual with the colored bands, and such a complete set. **Left to right:** sugar, crystal, $5; goblet with platinum ring, $10; creamer, $5.

PETALWARE

MacBeth-Evans Glass Company, 1930-1940
Colors: monax, cremax, pink, crystal, cobalt and fired-on red, blue, green, and yellow

The production of this opaque, hand painted glassware was intended to resemble ceramics. It is a very versatile design, some pieces having hand applied colored bands. Some have simple floral motifs. The dinner plates have a center design of concentric circles, surrounded by a wide band of plain glass, a circle inside the rim with fine scalloped edges.

This delicate Petalware was first produced in "Rose Pink" and crystal at the MacBeth-Evan factory in 1930.

The color monax was introduced in 1932. This color is a translucent, bluish white with some pieces having a gold trim. Later, a cream colored variation known as cremax was produced. Some are plain and some have concentric circles. More varieties of Petalware were introduced in the year 1936. Decorative hand painting was added to the monax and cremax. Three pastel bands—pink, blue, and green, some with just a gold band—and then floral designs in bright colors, fruits, flowers, and birds became popular. Not much of this decorated Petalware is seen in this area.

My first collection of this pattern was in monax, as it was inexpensive and looked attractive on colored placemats or tablecloths. I would say that Petalware in the variety of bright colors and the fragile and distinct designs is a highly versatile, coveted pattern.

Petalware. Plate, 8", salad, monax with decorated flower, $10; Plate, 8", salad, monax with decorated fruit, $10.

Petalware ribbon trim with fruits. **Left to right:** plate, 8", Lucretia Dewberry; plate, 8", Florence Cherry; plate, 8", Raspberry Strawberry; plate, 8", Muscat, $35-$40 each, scarce.

Petalware bluebird decorated plates. **Left to right:** plate, 8", $35-$40; plate, 8", $35-$40; plate, 11", $50; plate, 8", $35-$40; plate, 8", $35-$40.

Petalware. **Left to right:** sugar, $12; cup, $10; saucer, $4; creamer, $13, monax, decorated.

Petalware, MacBeth-Evans Glass Co., 1930-1940. This is beautiful glassware that resembles ceramics. The floral decorated is especially appealing. Plates, 6", sherbet, $3 each, monax with gold trim.

HOBNAIL

Hocking Glass Company, 1934-1936
Colors: crystal, crystal with red trim, and pink

This pattern is an adaptation of a traditional glass pattern. The centers of the plates consist of radial lines in a sunburst effect. The rims have raised dots or hobnails.

Other Depression Glass companies produced patterns with hobnail similarities. Hocking's Hobnail pattern is more distinct in its design, more like Moonstone's pattern that came out in 1942. The old hobnail molds were used, plus many new ones. In the Moonstone pattern, the hobs are white, producing the opalescent effect on the rims with a bluish white.

In pink, just a few pieces were produced, such as the 8-1/2" plate, 6" saucer, or sherbet plate, sherbet, and the cup. The pink color was called "Rose Glass" and the production of this color was discontinued in 1936. This glassware was produced especially for premiums.

Very striking is the crystal with the red trim, which captures the eye of most collectors. There is a great demand for these red trimmed pieces. The problem is their availability. In the Midwest, very little of this is seen. I ask dealer after dealer if they have any and the usual answer is not with the red trim but the plain untrimmed. The plain is not too appealing but may be more attractive in a compete set with some color accents.

Hobnail, Hocking Glass Co., 1934-1936. This is a traditional pattern with the raised dots or hobnails. Many Depression Glass companies produced patterns of hobnails. Cup, $5; saucer, $2; tumbler, 9 oz. or 10 oz., water, $6.

Hobnail, crystal with red trim. **Left to right:** sherbet, $3; bowl, 5-1/2", cereal, $4; plate, 8-1/2", luncheon, $4; cup, $5; saucer, $2, very striking.

JUBILEE AND ITS ACCESSORIES

This pattern, in the soft rich topaz color with the elegant flower and leaf design containing twelve petals with an open center, is admired by all glass lovers.

In spite of the scarcity and exorbitant prices for these pieces, the frantic search goes on—especially for the elusive accessories in this pattern. The basic luncheon set can be acquired with much patience and the willingness to pay the price. This basic set consists of the 8-3/4" luncheon plate, 7" salad plate, cup and saucer, sugar, creamer, tumbler 6", 10 oz. water, tray 11", two handled cake.

After acquiring the basic Jubilee set, a search for the serving pieces becomes a challenge, due to the scarcity, intense collector demand, and escalating prices.

Jubilee in pink has been discovered, although it is quite rare. Each of these pieces had the Jubilee open center flower etching with sixteen petals of even length. Collecting these pieces has become my goal.

Jubilee is a hand etched pattern. Therefore, we can assume that blanks from "related" patterns could be etched with Jubilee. Patrick, Jubilee's brother pattern, was a related pattern produced by Lancaster and made in topaz and rose. With the unidentified Jubilee pieces existing on Patrick blanks it is possible that any blank used for Patrick could have also been etched in Jubilee.

The Standard Glass Company, a Hocking division, received numerous colored blanks which were used for different patterns from Lancaster. Some of these "unrelated" patterns are collected as Jubilee.

Jubilee etchings were done on blanks that were also used for other patterns. This expanding of the original set of Jubilee pieces produced more of this exquisite pattern. The collector may find the Jubilee etching on one of these alternative blanks, which would make it a rare Jubilee piece. These pieces often command higher prices.

For all collectors of the extremely popular Jubilee pattern, it is significant to know that there are unreported or rare pieces of Jubilee. Knowing that these pieces exist makes it easier for the collector to decide whether to purchase the "unrelated" pieces, which can be costly.

Collecting the look-alike items is quite satisfying for many collectors, as the items can be cheaper and yet very elegant.

This set, produced by the Lancaster Glass Company in the early 1930s, represented the newest and most elaborate creation of modern glass production. Displaying and using a captivating luncheon set in Jubilee will charm any guest.

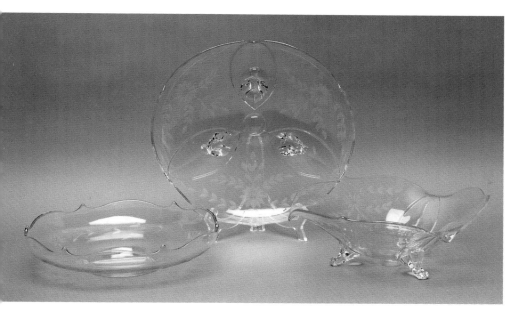

Jubilee, Lancaster Glass Co., early 1930s. This is an elegant and very delicately designed glassware in a soft yellow and pink. In yellow, the leaf design contains twelve petals with open center. **Left to right:** bowl, 11-1/2", flat fruit or plain bottom, part of the true set of Jubilee, $250; bowl, 11-1/2", 3 ftd., curved in with teardrop design, $250; bowl, 11" to 12", crimped, 3 ftd., $225. The pieces shown with teardrop shaped molding were etched with blanks that were used for the patterns Tyrus and Faith manufactured by the Standard Glass Manufacturing Co. of Lancaster, Ohio.

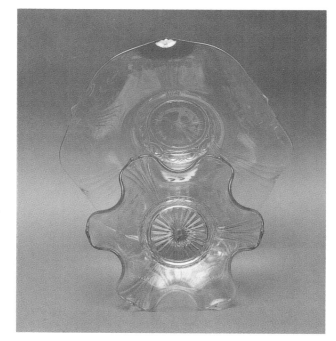

These exquisite pieces have the Jubilee design etched into the Lancaster blanks which were used for the pattern Sphinx. The bottom design is interlocking, no barth lines. **Top:** bowl, 12", flared out, $275. **Bottom:** bowl, 7-1/2" x 9", deeply crimped, 3 ftd., $275.

Pink Jubilee. This elusive color is becoming more and more scarce, very little is seen in the Midwest. Collecting this is my real challenge. **Left to right:** candy jar with lid, 3 ftd., $325; candy plate or bonbon, 3 ftd., $225; tray, 11", center handled, $200; plate, 13-1/2", sandwich, $90; bowl, 10-1/2", console, $275.

Jubilee. The cheese and cracker set, very attractive with the octagonal plate. A collector's dream. Set, $250.

Jubilee. These plates are from the Tyrus blank. **Left to right:** plate, 13", curved up, tear drop design, round, $225; plate, 14", pointed, tear drop design, flat, $250. **Center:** mayonnaise and plate with original ladle, $265.

Jubilee Stems. **Top row left to right:** 4-3/4", 4 oz., oyster cocktail, $75; stem, 7-1/2", 11 oz., $165; tumbler, 6-1/8", 12-1/2 oz., iced tea, $150; tumbler, 6", 10 oz., water, $33. **Bottom row left to right:** sherbet, champagne, 5-1/2", 7 oz., $95 (rare); stem, 4", 1 oz., cordial, $250 (rare).

"PATRICK," JUBILEE'S BROTHER PATTERN

This is a pattern about which we hear so little and yet it is so attractive. It is actually a brother pattern to the highly collected Jubilee, its sister pattern. It, too, is an elusive pattern with a masculine name but a feminine look.

Patrick has a delicate design of a three flowered bouquet in the center surrounded by flowers on either side of connecting leaves and vines. This floral pattern was typical for much of Lancaster's production.

Very little of this pattern is seen here in the Midwest, perhaps in other areas as well. I believe this to be a limited pattern due to the small production. The pink color in this pattern is very rare.

How I wish this pattern were more available, as it is an attractive set to accompany its sister pattern, "Jubilee." It looks as if Jubilee still reigns supreme. The serving pieces in Patrick are hard to find but some collectors go to the look-alikes, the plainer pieces.

I think we are becoming more aware of this scarce pattern due to its similarity to Jubilee. Serving pieces similar to Jubilee are rare. As a result of Patrick's scarcity, the prices are escalating.

Patrick. A very attractive pattern but very elusive. This floral pattern is typical of Lancaster Glass Co., early 1930s. **Left to right:** goblet, 6", 10 oz., water, $70; creamer, $38; plate, 8", luncheon, $28; sugar, $38.

CHILDREN'S SETS
ARE TREASURES

The glass dishes produced for the toy market during the Great Depression, so rare, expensive, and charming, have become a collector's dream. If you are searching for these sets, you may have to advertise widely to shops that specialize in them or get lucky at some antique shows and shops.

Many wonder why such sets were made of this breakable glassware. However, it was more of a tradition for the glassmakers in the 1920s and 1930s to carry on after producing children's toy dishes. Some ceramic companies had long before made plates in miniature for children's tea parties. As a result, many of these sets became popular throughout the nineteenth century for all doll furnishings and toys.

These sets of breakable dishes were actually produced as an additional line at a major manufacturing firm as an act of courtesy to the family service. The companies had to utilize the remainder of the materials at the end of the day and therefore produced these sets of dishes. This was a very unique and prudent method of production.

For children, it would be only natural to imitate their mothers' sets of dishes by arrangement and playing hostess. I can relate to this, remembering the many sets of these brightly colored dishes that I owned and used for playing house with my friends. Every Christmas I would receive boxes of these colored sets, beautifully wrapped. I would purchase a box of these unique dishes as a special gift for my friends.

The real purpose of the children's sets was for play purposes, creating a real sense of serving. These sets came in two sizes, one size for the child when serving her friends or for entertainment and the other size for playing with dolls.

Children's sets of dishes contained many colors, usually very bright with less clear or light colors.

One company, Akro Agate, was highly successful in producing sets of this glassware. The sets were boxed in various sizes and usually consisted of plates, cups, saucers, creamers, sugar bowls, and, in the larger sets, teapots with lids. These sets were made in the primary colors.

McKee Company made children's sets in French Ivory and Jade Green opaque glass. Some had embossed rims with motifs of berries or leaves. One group had a decal of a Scottie dog placed in the center of the plate in French Ivory.

Homespun, another pattern, has a children's set which is highly collectible. It was produced in crystal and pink. It consists of a cup, saucer, plate, teapot, and teapot cover. There is no sugar or creamer in this set. Interestingly, the teapot resembles a creamer with a lid like a sugar lid.

A very captivating set was made in cobalt blue in a block pattern. This had a lemonade pitcher and matching miniature tumblers. Wouldn't this be a treasure?

Glass companies did not distribute the children's sets themselves. In all likelihood they were boxed by toy manufacturers.

Collecting toy glass dishes of the Depression Era is a real challenge. The search may be fun, but difficult. Many of these sets were broken or discarded over the years; I know for a fact that mine were. In addition, many small cups and saucers found today are demitasse cups and these should not be confused with the toy market.

Children's sets are indeed a treasure to own. There is a great demand for them in spite of the rarity and high prices.

Moderntone, Platonite, Hazel Atlas Glass Co., early 1950s. "Little Hostess Party Dishes" are admired by doll dish collectors. Nothing excites one more than the bright combination of colors. The five popular sets range in color from pink/black/white top; lemon/beige/pink/ aqua; gray/rust/gold/turquoise; green/gray/chartreuse/burgundy; and pastel pink/green/blue/ yellow. Some of these colors are difficult to find; as a result, the prices increase. Interestingly, these toy dishes were a premium gift from Big Top Peanut Butter for a small fee. Some of the cups were souvenir gifts. **Back row left to right:** teapot, 3-1/2", brown, $80; with teapot lid, lemon, $80; teapot, burgundy, 3-1/2", $55; with teapot lid, burgundy, $60; teapot, bright pink, 3-1/2", $80; with teapot lid, black, $80; teapot, turquoise, 3-1/2", $62.50; with teapot lid, turquoise, $62.50. **Front row:** saucer, black, $12; cup, pink, $17.50; creamer, pink, $20; sugar, pink, $20; cup, lemon, $17.50; saucer, $7.

Cherry Blossom, Jeannette Glass Co., 1930-1939. This is a captivating, mold etched line that has been a very popular and attractive pattern with an all over floral design. In 1936, Cherry Blossom was produced in "Delphite," Jeannette's soft opaque blue. This adorable Child's Junior Dinner Set was also produced in the delicate pink color. **Right:** pink plate, 6", $12; sugar, $48; creamer, $48; cup, $37; saucer, $7. **Left:** Delphite plate, $13; creamer, $50; sugar, $50; cup, $40; saucer, $7. Pink, complete set, $325; Delphite, complete set, $350. A set consists of four plates, four cups, four saucers and a creamer and sugar.

Laurel, McKee Glass Co., 1930s. Children's Laurel Tea Sets are very popular and avidly sought. The Scotty Dog decorated in Jade Green and French Ivory is the most desired by collectors in this pattern. Prices have increased due to scarcity. The trimmed red and green in ivory is also becoming popular with collectors. **Back row left to right:** plate with green trim, $16; plate with red trim, $16. **Middle row left to right:** creamer with green trim, $40; sugar with green trim, $40. **Front row left to right:** cup with green trim, $30; saucer with green trim, $10; cup, plain, $20; cup with red trim, $30; saucer with red trim, $10.

Doric and Pansy, Jeannette Glass Co., 1937-1938. This pattern is very appealing with the predominant laurel leaf around on the dishes and a blocked rim border. Comes in the colors green, teal, pink, and some crystal. Jeannette Junior Dinner Set For Children, "Pretty Polly" Party Dishes, a fourteen piece set in the box. **Back row left to right:** plate, pink, $8; plate, teal, $10; (original box in the center). **Front row:** cup, pink, $35; saucer, $7; sugar, $35; creamer, $35; cup, teal, $45; saucer, $8.

UNIQUE PITCHERS AND PITCHER SETS

What could be more attractive and refreshing than a tall, beautifully designed pitcher of lemonade on a table surrounded by matching glasses on a hot, humid July day? Such an image was cherished back in the hard working days of the '30s and still is in the fast paced days of the '90s.

Different companies in the '30s gave various names to the pitchers, such as jugs, ball jugs and tilt jugs. Pitchers were produced in different shapes: square, tilt, round, squat (called a tilt jug), straight upright, fancy tankard, tilted juice with ice lip or without, the flat, the rounded bulbous type, and hexagonal.

Some patterns have three different styles of pitchers. These are the cone shaped with a round base with ice lip, a scalloped base footed with ice lip or without, and an all over pattern on the base. The cone shaped patterns are very characteristic of the Jeannette Glass Company from 1930-1938.

Decorated pitchers are beautiful with their etched designs. Patterns having the pitchers with the bands, crystal or decorated, are very attractive. Fostoria patterns have pitchers that are delicately decorated.

Floral and Diamond Band, U.S. Glass Co., 1927-1931. This was an early pattern of the deeply cut molded flower design. **Left to right:** pitcher, 8", 42 oz., $100; tumbler, 4", water, $25; tumbler, 5", iced tea, $45.

Manhattan, "Horizontal Ribbed," Anchor Hocking Glass Co., 1939-1941. Very attractive in pink in the horizontal sharp big rib design. Pitcher, 80 oz., tilted, $65.

Manhattan, "Horizontal Ribbed," Anchor Hocking Glass Co., 1939-1941. Pink tumblers, 10 oz., ftd., $17 each. Match the Manhattan tilted pitcher.

Wild Rose, Jeannette Glass Co., 1939. Pitcher, 80 oz., ice lip, tilt jug, $60.

The capacity of pitchers can vary from 16 to 96 ounces. The sizes can vary from 4-1/2" to 10-1/4". In some patterns, many pitchers were produced, ranging from the 23 ounce to the 80 ounce.

The handles on the pitchers are interesting to observe. Some are molded and some hand applied. Most of them are round and smooth, some have a ribbed effect, others are thick, long and narrow, some are square and pointed, and some ornately designed.

An interesting piece is the 8-1/2", 80 oz. pitcher in green for the price of $2,700 in the pattern, "Parrot," Sylvan by the Federal Glass Company, 1931-1932. I'm sure those who are fortunate enough to own one of these will keep it in their private collection. Also interesting is the pitcher and cover in the pattern, Old English, "Threading" by the Indiana Glass Company in the late 1920s. I would say this must be the most uniquely shaped of all the styles.

The seven piece pitcher sets, made in 1927, were designed to accommodate the new glass making machinery.

Floral, "Poinsettia" by the Jeannette Glass Company, 1931-1935 has a distinct lemonade pitcher, 10-1/4" and 48 oz.

I have seen ads from the '20s and '30s advertising a seven piece water set for just a couple of dollars. What a steal!

Today, we collectors search and search for these uniquely styled pitchers to complete our sets of glassware.

Florentine, No. 2, "Poppy No. 2," Hazel Atlas Glass Co., 1934-1936. This is a unique, cone-shaped pitcher with a center motif of flowers and scrolls in a pinwheel shape in yellow. Pitcher, 7-1/2", 28 oz., cone, ftd., $33.

Tilted pitchers were very popular in the '20s and '30s. Royal Ruby, 3 qt., tilted, $35; cobalt blue, fine ribbed, $35.

Royal Ruby, Anchor Hocking Glass Co., 1939-1960s. Very attractive set in the deep red color. Pitcher, 3 qt., upright, $40; tumblers, water, $7 each.

Forest Green, Anchor Hocking Glass Co., 1950s-1967. A rich green color in a later pattern but very popular and becoming scarce. Pitcher, 36 oz., $25; tumblers, water, $7 each.

Forest Green, Anchor Hocking pitcher, 22 oz., $23; tumblers, juice, $4 each.

Iris, "Iris and Herringbone," Jeannette Glass Co., 1928-1970. A highly collectible pattern in the Depression Glass field with the Iris flower and rayed bottom. Pitcher, 9-1/2", ftd., $38; tumblers, 6", ftd., $18 each.

Popular pitcher of the '30s. 8", $35; tumblers, 9 oz., $9 each.

Bubble, "Fire-King," Hocking Glass Co., 1934-1965. This pattern in red is becoming very popular and very scarce, and is increasing in price. Pitcher, 64 oz., ice lip, $55; tumbler, 12 oz., $13; tumbler, 16 oz., $16; tumbler, 12 oz., $13.

Ring, "Banded Rings," Hocking Glass Co., 1927-1933. This is an attractive crystal pitcher with decorated colors. 8-1/2", 80 oz., $33.

Below:
Ring, "Banded Rings," Hocking Glass Co., 1927-1933. Pitcher and set of glasses in crystal with the decorated colors. **Top row left to right:** goblet, 7-1/4", 9 oz., $15; pitcher, 8", 60 oz., $25; tumbler, 6-1/2", ftd., iced tea, $15. **Bottom row left to right:** tumbler, 3-1/2", 5 oz., $7; tumbler, 5-1/8", 12 oz., $10; tumbler, 4-1/4", 9 oz., $10; tumbler, 4", 8 oz., old-fashioned, $7; whiskey, 2", 1-1/2 oz., $10; tumbler, ftd., 5-1/2", water, $10.

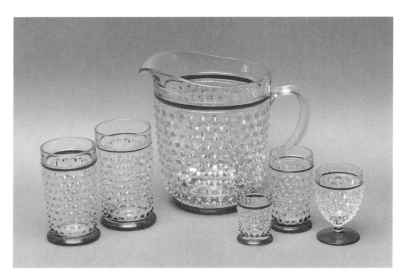

Hobnail, Hocking Glass Co., 1934-1936. Pitcher and glasses in red-trimmed crystal Hobnail, very striking. These are harder to obtain. **Left to right:** tumbler, water, 9 oz., $8; tumbler, water, 10 oz., $9; pitcher, 67 oz., $31; whiskey, 1-1/2 oz., $9; tumbler, juice, 5 oz., $6; tumbler, ftd., wine, 3 oz., $10.

"Ships" or "Sailboat," also known as "Sportsman Series," Hazel Atlas Glass Co., late 1930s. This pattern in "Ships" decorated Moderntone is not easy to collect. Some of the pieces like sherbet plates are exceedingly hard to find, especially in mint condition, perfect white design. **Top row left to right:** ice bowl, $35; pitcher with lip, 86 oz., $70; pitcher without lip, 82 oz., $60; plate, 5-7/8", sherbet, $28. **Front row left to right:** tumbler, 4-5/8", 9 oz., $11; tumbler, 6 oz., roly poly, $10; bowl, 4-1/4", $25; tumbler, 5 oz., 3-3/4", juice, $12; tumbler, 4 oz., heavy bottom, $27.50; tumbler, 4 oz., 3-1/4", heavy bottom, $27.50.

Popular tilted pitchers. **Left to right:** Waterford "Waffle," Hocking Glass Co., 1938-1944. A very distinctive pattern with the lattice or waffle design and radial sunburst lines. Pitcher, juice, 42 oz., tilted, $24. Manhattan, "Horizontal Ribbed," Anchor Hocking Glass Co., 1939-1941. A popular pattern in the horizontal sharp rib design. Pitcher, 42 oz., tilted, $32.

Manhattan, "Horizontal Ribbed," Anchor Hocking Glass Co., 1936-1943. Pitcher, 80 oz., tilted, crystal, $45; tumblers, 10 oz., ftd., $17 each.

Waterford "Waffle," Hocking Glass Co., 1938-1944. An attractive set in the waffle design. Tumblers are becoming scarce. Pitcher, 80 oz., ice lip, tilted, $33. Tumblers, 4-7/8", 10 oz., ftd., $13 each.

Windsor, "Windsor Diamond," Jeannette Glass Co., 1932-1946. An attractive pattern with diamond shaped facets. Pitcher, 4-1/2", 16 oz., $25; tumblers, 3-1/4", 5 oz., $8 each.

Bubble, "Fire-King," Hocking Glass Co., 1934-1965. This is a favorite pattern of many collectors with the scalloped edges and radial sunburst ending in a circle of bull's eye dots. Pitcher, 64 oz., ice lip, $60 (scarce and increasing in price); tumblers, 9 oz., water, $5 each.

Mayfair, "Open Rose," Hocking Glass Co., 1931-1937. This is a popular pattern with the center circle of roses and widely spaced lines. Pitcher, 6", 37 oz., $20.

DISTINCTIVE BUTTER DISHES

Another basic item of dinnerware sets produced in the Depression was the butter dish. This was part of the focal point of table settings, along with the creamer, sugar, salt and pepper shakers. It was usually placed in the center of the table. Actually, we still do this today but the butter dishes are not so elaborate or coordinated.

At one time I was thinking of collecting butter dishes but I realized this would have been quite a challenge as so many of the tops became chipped or broken due to the daily usage. Now they have become rare and very expensive. I have found the bottoms accidentally for quite a few and as of yet have not located the tops.

Butter tops were sold as butter holders in the old ice boxes. The tops slid into a metal holder, eliminating the need for a glass bottom.

The dome shaped butter dishes have always intrigued me and appear to be the popular style in most of the patterns.

Butter dishes were called preserve dishes in Hocking catalogues. In the pattern, Patrician, the butter bottom without the indented ledge is actually a jam dish.

Some butter bottoms are interchangeable, fitting other patterns. This is typical of the butter dishes produced by the U.S. Glass Company in the late 1920s. The bottoms produced are plain and can therefore be used for the patterns like Floral and Diamond Band, Cherryberry, and Strawberry. All of the tops are decorated in these patterns.

Left: Indiana Custard, "Flower and Leaf Band," Indiana Glass Co., early 1930s. A difficult pattern to collect due to the scarcity. Very attractive in the flower and leaf design in the rich ivory color. Butter dish and cover, $60. **Right:** Chinex Classic, MacBeth-Evans Division of Corning Glass Works, late 1930s early 1940s. A very distinctive looking butter dish with the brown castle design inside the base of the butter and the blue "pie crust" edge. Cover is plain with a blue edge. Butter dish bottom, $50; butter dish top, $45.

The first butter dish I found was in the pattern Columbia. I saw quite a few of these in the antique stores afterwards so I'm thinking this could be more common or perhaps a promotional item. Some can be found flashed with color and satinized.

Confusing to me are the cheese dishes and the butter dishes. There's a slight difference in the sizes of the lid and the bottom of both. This presented a problem to me when I found this item in the pattern, Sharon, "Cabbage Rose". In some patterns there are two styles of butter dishes.

Later on, in the '40s and '50s, the rectangular type of butter dish was produced, approximately 7-1/2" x 2 1/8", 1 lb. capacity, and the oblong, 1/4 lb. capacity. The round and oval along with the dome shaped were still produced.

For those not familiar with the butter dish in the Adam pattern, the butter dish combination with Sierra pattern is priced at $1,250. Can you envision having this in your collection? What a prize!

Left: Windsor, "Windsor Diamond," Jeannette Glass Co., 1936-1946. An attractive pressed pattern designed to imitate cut crystal. Consists of four larger bands of diamond shaped facets emanating from a circle of radial ribs. Butter dish, $28. **Right:** Dewdrop, Jeannette Glass Co., 1953-1956. This is a more recent pattern, attractive with the panels of fine beading and ribbed lines emanating from the knob to the bottom of the lid. Butter dish with cover, $28.

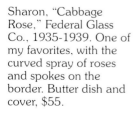

Sharon, "Cabbage Rose," Federal Glass Co., 1935-1939. One of my favorites, with the curved spray of roses and spokes on the border. Butter dish and cover, $55.

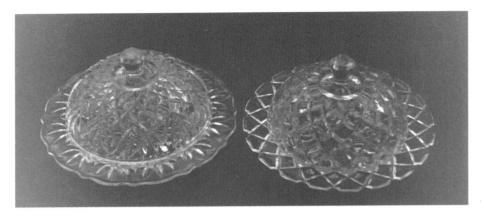

Left: Pressed glass with petal design produced in the 1930s. Butter dish with cover, $25.
Right: Waterford "Waffle," Hocking Glass Co., 1938-1944. An attractive pressed pattern with a lattice or waffle design and radial sunburst lines. Butter dish and cover, $25.

"Northwood" Co., 1920s, Wheeling, West Virginia, Regal, green opal with gold trim produced in the late 1920s, $175-$180. A favorite of mine.

Columbia Federal Glass Co.. 1938-1942. This butter dish was one of the first ones I found. It seems to be more available in this pattern. Attractive with the large beading inside the rim and the outer rim decorated with radial rows of graduated circles. Bottom of dish is square. Butter dish and cover, $20.

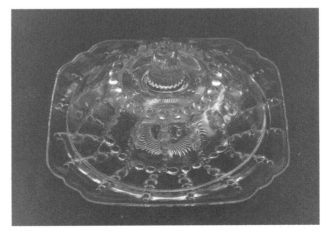

VERSATILE SERVING PIECES

As I started to collect Depression Glass and became more familiar with the patterns, I was amazed at the various serving pieces that were produced in the Depression Era. In many patterns, these were included to complete the sets. I am especially fond of the center handled servers, the sandwich, which are very distinctive and range in size from 11-12 inches. The shapes these servers can be found in are round, scalloped, octagon, and some square.

The other centered handled servers are also round, scalloped, octagon, and some square. They are the cake tray 10", a pastry 12", a fruit 12", a lunch 11", a bon bon tray 7-1/2", and a handled nut bowl. These were produced in the 1930s. The McKee and Lotus companies plus other smaller companies were big producers of these servers.

The handles of these servers can be very ornate, some closed and some open. Each is unique in its own design.

When I was researching these center handled servers, I came across the Cameo, "Ballerina" or "Dancing Girl" in green with the shocking, exorbitant price of $5,500.00. Wouldn't this be a challenge and indeed a treasure if one could luck into this? I'm afraid this will never be in my possession unless the flea market, an estate sale, or auction would reveal this "find."

All of my servers are put to good use for serving cookies, sandwiches, and all kinds of snacks. They are the most convenient and attractive for serving guests. Right now I am searching for more of these handsome and useful servers.

Grill and chop plates still remain popular with some collectors. Besides their use in separating food, these divided plates are also ideal for serving snacks. Both

Imperial Glass Co., Bellaire, Ohio, early 1920s-1930s. This company produced an elegant line of fine engraved designs in various pieces. Bonbon tray, 7-1/2" to 8" in pink with the center handle, $35-$40.

grill plates and chop plates are typical of the Depression Era. The chop plates are used for serving assortments of cookies, bars, other desserts, sandwiches, rolls, and hors d'oeuvres. They can be used for any type of dinner, luncheon, or breakfast.

The two, three, and four part relish plates, so popular in many of the patterns, are also useful in serving. The small bowls, 5-1/2" to 6-1/2", one handled and deep or center handled, are ideal to use as well.

All of these versatile serving pieces were made to represent the eating habits of the United States during an interesting time in our history.

Imperial Glass Co., Bellaire, Ohio, early 1920s-1930s. This company produced elegant glassware with fine hand cutting on highly polished crystal. Sandwich tray, 11", $30.

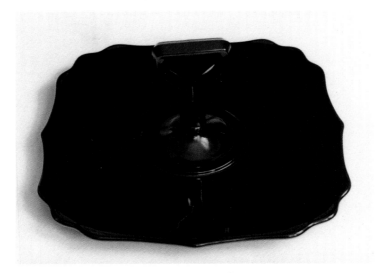

"Charade" pattern produced in the 1920s and 1930s. Sandwich server, 10", slightly pointed and ruffled edging, $40.

Bubble, "Fire-King," Hocking Glass Co., 1934-1965. This is an easy pattern to identify with the scalloped edges and centers with radial sunbursts ending in a circle of bull's eye dots. Plate, 9-3/8", grill, $24, blue. Finding this requires a long, hard search.

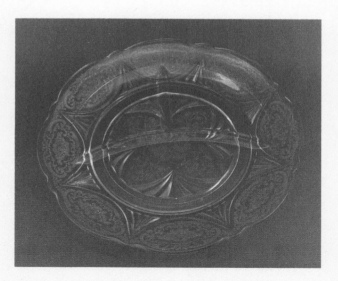

Royal Lace, Hazel Atlas Glass Co., 1934-1941. An outstanding mold etched pattern with the motif of lacy scrolls, leaves and flowers surrounded by a drape design. Plate, 9-7/8", grill, crystal, $11.

Rosemary, "Dutch Rose," Federal Glass Co., 1935-1937. A
simple but very appealing pattern to collectors with the
center bouquet of roses and the rim of roses placed between
overlapping, looped designs. Plate, 9-1/4", grill, pink, $25.
Very difficult to find.

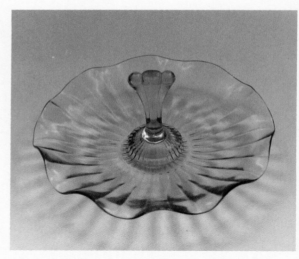

Anchor Hocking Glass Co., 1930s, handled mint tray,
7-1/4", $22. Ray designed and ruffled edges.

Old Colony, "Lace Edge," "Open Lace," Hocking Glass
Co., 1935-1938. This is a well-known pattern among
veteran Depression Glass collectors. Very unique in this
pressed pattern with a pierced or open border design.
Top plate, 8-3/4", luncheon, $24; bottom plate, relish, 3
part, $26.

Mt. Pleasant "Double Shield," L.E. Smith Co.,
1920s-1934. An easy pattern to identify with
the alternating indentations and points.
Bonbon, 6", center handle, $25, very popular
in the '20s and '30s. Ideal for serving mints.

No. 618, Pineapple and Floral, Indiana Glass Co., 1932-1937. This is a pressed pattern in the sandwich glass tradition. Center motif is a flower surrounded by a pineapple type pressed design with a floral border. Plate, 11-1/2", sandwich, crystal, $18. An ideal serving piece.

Swirl, "Petal Swirl," Jeannette Glass Co., 1937-1938. A favorite pattern of this company in ultramarine. It has a motif of concentric ribbed circles and an outer rim of swirled ribs on the border. Plate, 12-1/2", sandwich, $30. A very attractive serving piece in this color.

Swirl, "Petal Swirl," Jeannette Glass Co., 1937-1938. Very attractive with the swirled ribs and scalloped top. Candy dish, open, 3 legs, $14.

Imperial Glass Co., Bellaire, Ohio, 1920s-1930s. This company produced a great variety of utilitarian wares in special colors. Candy box with cover, 5-1/4", $30. Very unique in rose-pink.

Left: Fortune, Hocking Glass Co., 1937-1938. Plain pattern with widely spaced radial ridges emanating from the center to a border of wider panels divided by straight radial lines. Bowl, 4-1/2", handled, $9. **Center:** Oyster and Pearl, Anchor Hocking Glass Co., 1938-1940. A plain pattern with a center sunburst surrounded by a circle of more widely spaced radiating lines. Bowl with handles, closed, $8. **Right:** Bowl, 4-1/2", handled, Fortune, $9.

Oyster and Pearl, Anchor Hocking Glass Co., 1938-1940. Very unique in its styling of rays, large and small beading, circular loops, and slightly ruffled edging. Relish dish, 10-1/4", oblong, divided, $14.

Windsor, "Windsor Diamond," Jeannette Glass Co., 1932-1946. A pressed pattern resembling cut crystal. Consists of a series of larger bands of diamond shaped facets emanating from a circle of radial ribs. Relish platter, 11-1/2", divided, $15.

Royal Lace, Hazel Atlas Glass Co., 1934-1941. Very attractive in crystal with the motif of lacy scrolls, leaves and flowers, surrounded by a draped design. Plate, 9-7/8", grill, $12.

Sandwich, Indiana Glass Co., 1920s-1980s. An attractive set with the all over stippling spaced around flower, foliage, and scroll motifs in an elaborate arrangement. Bowl, 6", mayonnaise, ftd., with ladle, $15; plate, 7", $4.

Windsor, "Windsor Diamond," Hocking Glass Co., 1932-1946. An ideal serving bowl, 7-1/8", 3 legs, $8.

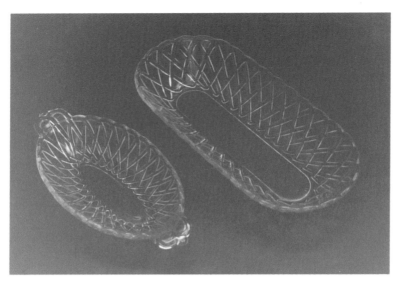

Pretzel, Indiana Glass Co., 1930s. This is a unique pattern with crossed or x-shaped ribs and rounded edges. **Left to right:** bowl, 8-1/2", 2 handled, pickle, $6; bowl, 10-1/4", celery, $2.

Pretzel, Indiana Glass Co., 1930s. **Left to right:** a unique fruit set. Plate, 6", tab handled, $3; bowl, 4-1/2", fruit cup, $5; bowl, 7", olive, leaf shaped, $5.

Left: Pretzel, Indiana Glass Co., 1930s. Plate, 7-1/4", square, indent, 3 part, $10; **Right:** "Daisy," No. 620, Indiana Glass Co., 1933. Crystal relish dish, 8-3/8", 3 part, $12.

THE DECORATED SWANKY SWIGS
1930s - EARLY 1940s

Every time my friends and guests view these decorated glasses they question the origin and the name given to them. Many remember seeing and using them before but had no idea that they had become such a unique collectible. They become very interested in the history of them.

In the advertising department of the Kraft Company in the early 1930s, the Vice President, John H. Pratt, came up with the idea of a reusable tumbler for the company's cheese products, a cheese spread. After a little research, the Swanky Swig came into being and became so popular in 1933.

So many ask why were they called this name. Actually, there isn't an exact reason for this fascinating title except that they were a decorated tumbler that became a party type name.

These glasses containing the various cheese spreads became very popular with the housewives of the Depression Era. Used at breakfast for juices, the brightly decorated glasses truly enlivened the table in those depressing days. I can vividly recall these glasses, as my family purchased many varieties of the cheese spreads. The glasses fascinated me, but as was the custom back then, they were discarded. Surprisingly, I use them now and enjoy collecting them for juice glasses. My family is en-

Swanky Swigs, 1930s to early 1940s. Band Pattern was the first pattern in a simple band design that was hand applied. **Left to right:** No. 1, red and black, 3-3/8", $2-$3; No. 3, white, hairline at top and bottom with two blue bands, 3-3/8", $3-$4; No. 4, two 1/16", blue bands with a 3/32" space between them, 3-3/8", $3-$4; Circles and Dot, random design of concentric circles with a small dot in the center, red, 3-1/2", $4-$5; blue, 3-1/2", $3-$4; Stars, No. 1, random design of various sized stars, red, 3-1/2", $3-$4; green, 3-1/2", $3-$4; black, 3-1/2", $3-$4. **Center:** Band Pattern, No. 2, alternate bands of black and red, black at the top, 3-3/8", $2-$3.

thralled with them, especially my grandchildren, and they are put to good use. All of us enjoy the hunt for Swanky Swigs—finding some of them is a real challenge.

Swanky Swigs became a real hit as a premium item and won an award for the Kraft Company.

Other companies, Hazel Atlas and the White Cap, started to produce these tumblers as well and had them on the store shelves in 1933. They had a top-sealing cap. However, only the Kraft glasses are the true "Swanky Swigs." There are glasses that have the look of the Swanky Swig but are referred to only as the "Look-alikes." The common size is 3-1/2", and the larger ones are 4-1/2" to 4-3/4".

The first pattern on the Swanky Swigs was a simple band design which was hand applied. Later, more decorating motifs came about and each one became more elaborate and inventive. In 1937, the original tulip came out, the most popular. People seemed to prefer the flower type. In 1939, the trend was for brightly colored dinnerware, so for a short time Kraft introduced the carnival tumbler in colors of orange, yellow, blue, green, and red.

The Years Swanky Swigs Were Produced

Band Pattern	1934-1935	Posy Pattern Cornflower No. 1	1941
Circles and Dot	1934	Posy Pattern Cornflower No. 2	1947
Stars	1935	Forget-Me-Not	1948
Checkerboard	1936	Tulip No. 3	1950
Sailboat No. 1	1936	Crystal Petal	1951
Sailboat No. 2	1936	Bustlin' Betsy	1953
Texas Centennial	1936	Antique No. 1	1954
Tulip No. 1	1937	Bachelor Button	1955
Carnival	1939	Kiddie Kup	1956
Posy Pattern Jonquil	1941	Hostess Design	1960
Posy Pattern Violet	1941	Colonial	1976
Posy Pattern Tulip	1941		

Swanky Swigs. **Left to right:** Tulip, No. 1, tulips and pots are colored with leaves, white on each glass, red, 3-1/2", $3-$4; Posy Pattern, Tulip, red tulips with green leaves, red/green, 3-1/2", $4-$5; Posy Pattern, Jonquil, yellow jonquil with green leaves, yellow/green, 3-1/2", $5-$6; Tulip, No. 1, blue, 3-1/2", $3-$4; Posy Pattern, Cornflower, No. 2. On this design the leaves and flowers are the same color, light blue, 3-3/16" to 3-1/2", $2.50-$3.50. Checkerboard, an all over checkerboard with white at the top on each glass, white/red, 3-1/2", $25-$28; Tulip, No. 1, 3-1/2", black, $3-$4; Posy Pattern, Violet, blue violets with green leaves, blue/green, 3-1/2", $5-$6; Forget-Me-Not, two rows of similarly colored flowers with a row of green leaves at the bottom, dark blue, 3-1/2", $2.50-$3.50; Posy Pattern, Cornflower, No. 1, light blue flowers with green leaves, 3-1/2", $4-$5. **Center:** Sailboat, No. 1, three sailboats as shown appear on this glass, blue, 3-1/2", $10-$12.

Left to right: Swanky Swigs Bustlin' Betsy, a series featuring the Maid Betsy performing various household duties, yellow, 3-3/4", $5-$6; Hostess Design, a plainware glass round at the top with a square base and molded flutes and leaf design at the bottom, 3-3/4", $2.50-$3.50; Kiddie Kup, a series of animals and toys with a band of small white animals around the top, blue, 3-3/4", $4-$5; Colonial, plainware glass design consists of molded waffle-like bands around the glass, 3-3/4", $2-$3; Antique, No. 1, a series of designs showing various early American antiques, 3-3/4", $4-$5; Crystal Petal, plainware glass with a row of 24 molded flutes at the bottom, 3-1/2", $2.50-$3.50; Bachelor Button, a pattern with a top row of red daisies plus a white row in the middle and a row of green leaves at the bottom, 3-3/4", $2-$3. Coin Design, a plainware glass with a series of coin-like indentations around the bottom, 3-3/4", $2.50-$3.50; Tulip No. 3, a colored flower with green leaves on each glass and 4 molded bands around the top, 3-3/4", $2-$3. The smaller size (3-1/4") and the larger size (4-1/2"), are less available in this area.

Everyone has a favorite decorated style, the star, circle and dot, checkers, sailboat, kiddy cup, flowers, Bustling Betsy, or Antique. What's mine? The Bustling Betsy with her activities and the Antique Patterns portraying the coffee grinder and plate, spinning wheel and bellows, coffee pot and trivet, churn and cradle, clock and coal scuttle, lamp and kettle—all fascinate me. These came in sharply colored yellow, brown, blue, green, and red.

If you are searching for Swanky Swigs, check rummage sales and flea markets.

Children appear to be fascinated by them and become avid collectors themselves. My granddaughter Jamie and my two neighbor boys, Teddy and Tyler, are among them.

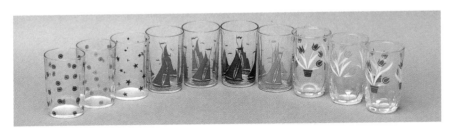

Swanky Swigs. **Left to right:** Circles and Dot, black, 3-1/2", $5-$6; Circles and Dot, green, 3-1/2", $5-$6; Star, 4-3/4", blue, $8-$10; Sailboat, No. 2, red, 3-1/2", $12-$15; Sailboat, No. 2, green, 3-1/2", $10-$15; Sailboat, No. 2, blue, 3-1/2", $10-$12; Sailboat, No. 2, light green, 3-1/2", $10-$15; Tulip No. 1, red, 3-1/2", $3-4; Tulip No. 1, yellow, 3-1/2", $3-4; Tulip No. 1, green, 3-1/2", $3-4.

Swanky Swigs. **Left to right:** Texas Centennials, black, 3-1/2", $32.50-$35; green, 3-1/2", $32.50-$35; Texas cobalt, 4-3/4", $32.50-$35; Texas Centennials, blue, 3-1/2", $32.50-$35; red, 3-1/2", $32.50-$35; Checkerboard, 3-1/2", blue, $25-$27.50; Checkerboard, 3-1/2", green, $25-$27.50; Carnival, blue, red, green, yellow, 3-1/2", $5-$7. There are Swanky Swigs and "Look-alikes." Only the Kraft glasses are the "true" Swanky Swigs.

POST PROHIBITION GLASSWARE

In 1933, when Prohibition was repealed, the Depression Era glassmakers had a new market. Alcoholic beverages could be legally served and the glassmakers immediately began making decanters, cocktail and martini shakers, cocktail and bar glasses of all sizes, ice buckets, punch bowls, cups, and other utensils for the service of liquor. Many of these were made in familiar patterns to match the dinnerware sets.

The decanter sets were very attractive with the unique decanter usually surrounded by six brilliant glasses with their bands of gleaming platinum. The platinum stayed bright because of the specially crafted application. The ritz blue or black with the crystal stopper was very striking with the bright platinum decoration.

Hazel Atlas Company is most responsible for the glass cocktail shakers of the 1930s. That company made modern blue glass containers with decals in white of sailboats, golfers, and horses with riders. These were called the "Sportsman Series" and are avidly sought today. Especially collectible are the shakers and a matching set of glasses. There are glasses with miniature motifs matching those found on the cocktail shakers that are somewhat difficult to find in quantity. The shakers themselves were made of heavy glass and seemed to survive. Glasses got a great deal more handling since they were used for other than alcoholic drinks and many more broke.

Federal was the biggest supplier of machine made tumblers, jugs, and decanters. The beverage glasses they produced were very unique.

Hobnail, Hocking Glass Co., 1934-1936, an adaptation of a traditional glass pattern. The hobs and radial lines in a sunburst effect are characteristic of this pattern. Rims have raised dots. Decanter and Stopper, 32 oz., $30; tumblers, ftd., wine, 3 oz., $7 each.

Ring, "Banded Rings," Hocking Glass Co., 1927-1933. This is an early pattern called Circle Design, consisting of horizontal ribbed bands in a circle pattern. Crystal decorated with yellow, red, and black enamel rings, very attractive, was produced a little later. Decanter and Stopper, $27; tumblers, 3" to 3-1/2", $5 each.

The Jeannette Company and Indiana Company were big producers of ice tubs and beverage glasses.

There were other companies that produced these items but not as profusely as those above. Some patterns from these companies did not have any of these sets. Dunbar's specialties over the years were the refreshment sets, liquor services, and cocktail sets with shakers.

Remember the popular Servette Sets, the four, five, or six piece tray and handle with various size tumblers? Another set contained the quart size cocktail shaker, ice tub and tongs, six tumblers, and tray. These sets were produced in colors and the utensils were genuine silver plated. There were sandwich trays as well as cracker and cheese dishes, ideal for serving purposes.

Some liquor sets have 1-3/4 oz. glasses in various colors: amber, green, blue, and amethyst. The etched designs were very attractive and rich looking.

Wine sets were produced with low stemmed glasses of 3 oz. capacity. Fancy stoppers were ground in the decanters.

Whiskey decanters on stands, shaped like kegs, were part of sets used in the '30s. Many came with trays and matching glasses. The whiskey was poured through an opening in the top and measured into the glasses through a spigot in the side.

Glasses of all sizes for every known mixed or unmixed drink were produced. Some were made in major Depression Glass sets or highball sets which came with their own trays.

Ice cubes came out of the new electric refrigerators and were then stored in the new glass ice buckets.

The "Tom and Jerry" mug sets in porcelain were produced in this era by Hazel Atlas and the McKee Glass Companies. They were actually made of white opaque glass and were hot-punch sets, heat proof to hold hot punch. Due to only limited usage on the holidays many of these sets survived in good condition. They were decorated in a variety of colorful decals, some with a Christmas motif.

The elegant and useful punch bowl sets were introduced during this period. A Moderntone punch set in ritz blue, a different style, was sold in the '30s. The glass insert is cobalt blue and the holder a shiny chrome-plated metal. There were other traditional designs in inexpensive glass punch sets of the Depression period. However, the blue glass and chrome sets were typical of this era. The punch bowl consists of the large bowl, a base, twelve cups, and ladle.

What American custom resulted from this era? Can you guess? It was the birth of the "American Happy Hour," or commonly known today as just "Happy Hour." The cocktail, an American drink taken before dinner, was highly glamorized in cookbooks that featured numerous recipes for mixed drinks and cocktails in the 1930s. The cocktail is still very much glamorized among American people today.

Decanters, bottle sets, cocktail shakers, ice buckets, and a great variety of glasses were made to welcome the end of Prohibition. Given the variety of shapes, sizes, and colors from the glassmakers' new market, one could rejoice and sing the familiar song, "Happy Days Are Here Again." How many remember that song?

Ring, "Banded Rings," Hocking Glass Co., 1927-1933. Cocktail shakers, crystal, decorated with chrome tops in three different styles, $30 each.

Ring, "Banded Rings," Hocking Glass Co., 1927-1933. Decanters, crystal, decorated, $42 each.

Fenton Art Glass, Williamston, West Virginia 1930. Georgian, 8 oz., tumblers with heavy bottoms in green, red, and cobalt blue, $8 each. Ideal for serving beverages.

Right:
Hazel Atlas Glass Co., 1930s, cocktail shaker in a deep red, banded bottom, heavy chrome plated top, 11", $50-$55.

Hocking Glass Co.. 1927-1933. **Left to right:** "Boopie" tumbler, red with crystal bottom, 9 oz., $8; goblet, 8 oz., $20; "Boopie," tumbler, 9 oz., red with crystal bottom, $8.

Anchor Hocking Glass Co., 1927-1939. **Left to right:** Royal Ruby wine glass, 2-1/2", ftd., wine, $14; Georgian tumbler, 5 oz., $6; wine glass, ftd., $14.

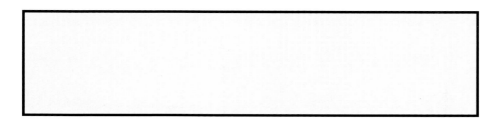

Ring, "Banded Rings," Anchor Hocking Glass Co., 1927-1932. Ice bucket with uniquely designed handles, crystal with colored banded rings, $35.

Old Oaken Bucket produced in the 1930s. Collectors gave this ice tub its name, due to the rough textured surface resembling wood. Ice tub, $25; matching 2 oz. liquor glasses, $1.50-$2.

New Martinsville Glass Manufacturing Co., New Martinsville, West Virginia, liquor set, apple green. Decanter, 6", ground in stopper with small spout, $25; matching liquor glasses, 2 oz., $2 each.

L.E. Smith Glass Co., 1920s-1934, cocktail tray, 15" x 6", $22; liquor glasses, 2 oz., $1.50-$2 each.

Greensburgh Glass Works, Greensburgh, Pennsylvania. This company was a big producer of the servette handled trays for serving beverages, 1920s-1930s. Tray, $15-$20; serving glasses, 6 oz., iridescent, $3-$4 each.

Greensburgh Glass Works, Greensburgh, Pennsylvania, Servette Set. Tray, handled, $15; serving glasses, 4 oz., $2.50-$3 each.

Seneca Glass Co., Morgantown, West Virginia, 1930s. This company produced the "slim" glassware line with round and square crystal feet in stemware. Wine glasses with crystal bottoms, 4 oz., $6-$8 each.

Hazel Atlas Glass Co., 1934-1942, Tom and Jerry Set, 9" bowl and punch cups with red and green trim. Made in opaque white in the 1940s, all marked H.A. Set with the six cups shown, $25. Perfect for the holidays with the Christmas motif.

Hazel Ware, Division of Continental Can, 1950s-1960s. This punch set complete (one of my first and favorites) is very elegant and similar to Alpine, a 15 piece punch set. Many sets were produced in the 1930s. On this set, the punch cups have open handles to hang onto the side of the punch bowl. Complete set, $35-$45.

RARE PIECES IN SOME PATTERNS

This chapter is not meant to be a complete history of the rare glassware in Depression Glass. Its intent, however, is to make collectors aware that there are certain rare pieces in the various patterns. If you are familiar with them and find them affordable, it would be worth your while to purchase them.

Again, it is imperative to know the pieces of the patterns so that you don't pass them up. I'm sure many of us have seen unfamiliar shapes or colors in some of the patterns we recognize but didn't realize they were rare. Imagine finding some of these rare pieces for a small fee and then discovering the true value of them. Wouldn't that be a real "find" to rejoice over?

"Parrot," Sylvan, Federal Glass Co., 1931-1932. This is a mold etched pattern distinctive of Depression Glass. The unusual design is a scenic pattern of parrots sitting on bamboo branches. Not only is it unusual in design, it is scarce, very desirable, and expensive. Hot Plate, 5", round, green, $900. A cherished piece, but difficult to find.

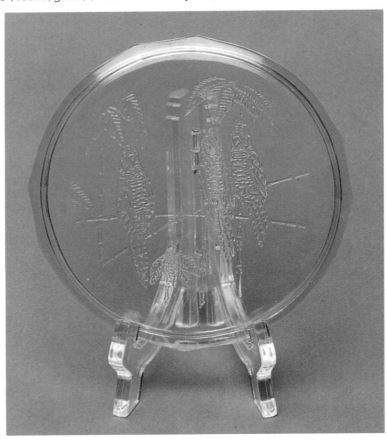

"Rock Crystal," Early American Rock Crystal, McKee Glass Co., 1920s-1930s. An attractive pattern with a five leaf flower surrounded by a wreath-like design and scrolls. An all over decorated pattern. Plate, 8-1/2", with plain edge in red, $25. More expensive and scarce in the color red.

Sunflower, Jeannette Glass Co., 1930s. This is a pattern especially appealing to collectors, with its stylized sunflower and foliage. Trivet, 7", 3 legs, turned up edge and 3" smaller than the common 10" cake plate, $320. The most elusive piece of sunflower is in pink.

Chinex Classic, MacBeth-Evans Division of Corning Glass Works, late 1930s early 1940s. The castle decal items with the blue trim, light and dark, are extremely popular and more difficult to find. **Back row left to right:** bowl, 6-3/4", salad, $40; plate, 9-3/4", dinner, $20; bowl, 9", vegetable, $40. **Bottom row left to right:** bowl, 5-3/4", cereal, $15; saucer, $6; cup, $15; plate, 6-1/4", sherbet, $8.

Chinex Classic, MacBeth-Evans Division of Corning Glass Works, late 1930s early 1940s. The castle decal bowls and plate in brown are very attractive and scarce. **Left to right:** bowl, 9", vegetable, $40; plate, 6-1/4", sherbet, $8; plate, 9-3/4", dinner, $20.

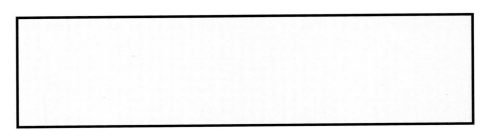

Starlight, Hazel Atlas Glass Co., 1938-1940. This is another unique pattern, with the center of the plate in a waffle design and the borders with cross-over stippled lines that give a plaid effect. Plate, 13", sandwich, $15; bowl, 11-1/2", salad, $25. Few of the 13" plates are being found and the bowl is becoming scarce as well. This is a popular set for salad.

Below:
No. 622, Pretzel, Indiana Glass Co., 1930s. These pieces in this pattern with the embossed fruits painted on the bottoms are more difficult to find but are attractive. Plate, 11-1/2", sandwich, $15; plate, 8-3/8", salad, $8.

Waterford "Waffle," Hocking Glass Co., 1938-1944. This is a Waterford "Waffle" tumbler shaped like the Miss America style. This Waterford patterned piece had the same mould shape as Miss America. $15-20.

Popular Sources of Collecting

Once plentiful, the glassware of the 1920s and 1930s is being picked up fast because the supply is dwindling and prices escalating. However, this glassware can be found at the right places at the right time.

As warm weather approaches, our thoughts turn to yard sales, garage sales, and flea markets. We are mobile people and traveling through towns we can spot these sales and also visit the antique shops. It is amazing what can be found, the "real finds." Remember to get to these places early if you want the choice and chance of getting a "sleeper." With the annual spring cleaning of attics and basements, some of this precious glassware will surface.

Flea markets are still very popular places to find pieces for your collections. So many dealers are eager to get rid of their excess glassware and among this you may find that one piece you are looking for. Also, they will negotiate with you. At these places I have been fortunate at finding the pieces to complete my sets.

Watch the local newspapers in your town for auctions. They are widely advertised and Depression Glass collectors are inveterate auction goers. There is always Depression Glass available when the owners of the house are trying to dispose of their property as they relocate.

New and used stores and charity shops like the Goodwill can reveal a treasure now and then, or even the "sleeper." I've always said that "Depression Glass" is in many respects "a sleeper."

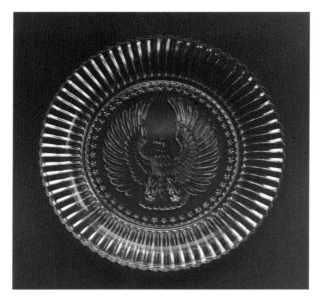

Plate, 8", in a brilliant crystal, $13. A unique garage sale find. Stars and Stripes, Anchor Hocking Glass Co., 1942. Plate resembles Queen Mary but is different with the inner circle of stars and the eagle in the center of the plate.

Another source is from your relatives and older people who may just want to get rid of their so called "old stuff" for just a small amount of money.

Depression Glass shows are very popular, as you get to view the whole array of all patterns, shapes, colors, and individual pieces at some fair prices. In the midst of the antiquing season, when all the dedicated antiquers hit the highways, much excitement and enthusiasm is generated among the various sales in full bloom. The die-hard collectors are anxious to get back in the swing. With the economy more stable and inflation down, collectors are more eager to search for and buy what they like. Interest in buying for their collections takes precedence over investment purposes—they aren't thinking so much of the potential value. I'm glad to see this is for preservation purposes.

Old Cafe, Hocking Glass Co., 1936-1940. This is a plain pattern with a center sunburst surrounded by a circle of more widely spaced radiating lines. There are wide panels with three narrow lined panels. Vase, 7-1/4", $20. An attractive garage sale find.

Below:
Ovide, Hazel Atlas Co., 1930-1935. Very little of this pattern is found in black. These cups match my luncheon set in yellow and black. Cup and saucer, $10 each. A good flea market find.

Georgian, Anchor Hocking Historical Classics Collection, 1930s, Lancaster, Ohio. **Left to right:** four juice glasses, 5-1/2 oz., mint in box, $20; four beverages, 9 oz., mint in box, $45. The perfect auction find.

American Sweetheart, MacBeth-Evans Glass Co., 1930-1936. Decorative pattern with design on the outside of festoons, ribbons, and scroll designs. Sherbet in a metal holder, $5. An unusual find at the Goodwill store.

"Bubble," "Bullseye," "Provincial," Anchor Hocking Glass Co., 1940-1965. Bowl, 5-1/2" wide and 3" deep, $5. Resembles the Bubble pattern except for the straight edge. An unusual find at the New and Used store.

Block Optic, "Block." This pattern has the typical 1930s look with the design and color. It contains wide concentric circles set off in blocks. Creamer, $13; sugar, $13. A perfect find for my set at the antique store.

"Bubble," "Bullseye," "Provincial," Anchor Hocking, 1940-1965. This item has the Bubble pattern, true Bubble, but is seen infrequently in the pink color. Bowl, 8-3/8", $8. An attractive find at the antique store.

DISPLAYING DEPRESSION GLASS

The joy of collecting this glassware, especially if you have sets in the various colors, is the display. The holidays are great for this and to me it is the most enjoyable part of my hobby. By displaying this glassware you become more familiar with it and can assist new collectors by demonstrating the numerous patterns and colors. It is truly enjoyable for veteran collectors and knowledgeable for novice collectors.

A group of cookie jars in numerous Depression Glass colors makes a handsome shelf display. I saw this recently and I was really impressed.

Lighted glass hutches and curios are the most convenient and attractive means of displaying your glassware. Colored glass looks the best under a good light. On the lighted mirrored shelf each glittering piece is just as beguiling as the next.

On glass topped tables the various pieces reflect their ethereal beauty. Another way to display the colored vases, bottles, and smaller items is on windowsills. Cobalt blue is especially attractive displayed in this manner.

Crystal, perhaps not as popular for color, is the perfect accessory for candies, assorted cheeses, pickles, meat cuts, cookies, and other snacks. The clear glass, some very decorative with etchings, blends in with all of the colored glassware.

Royal Ruby, Anchor Hocking Glass Co., 1939-1960s. Table setting in deep red, very festive for the Christmas holiday. **Center:** plate, 9" or 9-1/4", dinner, $11. **Left to right:** sherbet, ftd., $8; tumbler, 9 oz., water, $7; cup, $6; saucer, $3.

Colored cups on crystal saucers or crystal cups on colored saucers are pretty and fun to use. This proves how much you can do with the colored glassware. Most of my crystal pieces are put to good use for serving meals daily and for special occasions.

All of the glass patterns and colors, so new and exciting in the 1920s and 1930s, have once again become attractive accessories for our homes due to the recent Art Deco revival. It is a welcome to the enchantment of the "rainbow colors" so typical of Depression Glass.

Left: Princess, Hocking Glass Co., 1931-1935. The center motif is a snowflake with eight spokes, adorned with lines, flowers, and leaves. Cookie jar and cover, green, $60. **Right:** Mayfair, "Open Rose," Hocking Glass Co., 1931-1937. An attractive pattern with the center circle of roses, widely spaced lines, and scalloped edges. Cookie jar and lid, pink, $55.

Various colored cups on crystal saucers, a great way to display the colors. **Right to left:** hobnail, pink, cup on crystal saucer, cup, $10, saucer, $2; Block Optic, "Block," green, cup, $7; on a Waterford "Waffle" saucer, $2; Diana, amber, cup, $7; on a crystal saucer, $2.

I strongly feel that Depression Glass should be used and enjoyed. The more it is brought to the attention of the general public, the more it will be preserved and treasured. What better way to introduce Depression Glass than to use this glassware for serving guests. I use mine for serving guests, and believe me, it's a great hit and becomes a dream in your home.

Assorted vases in different colors, can be beautifully displayed on windowsills for holidays or decorating purposes. **Left to right:** ruffled top, amethyst, $22; slim with ruffled top in green, $11; slim with ruffled top in red, $11; ruffled top, cobalt blue, $22.

Forest Green, Anchor Hocking Glass Co., 1950s-1967. Table setting in bright green, also very festive for the Christmas holiday. **Center:** plate, 9-1/4", dinner, $30. **Left to right:** sherbet, $7; tumbler, 9 oz., $7; cup, $5; saucer, $2.

Moderntone, "Wedding Band," Hazel Atlas Glass Co., 1934-1942. **Left to right:** cream, soup, 5", $34; plate, 8-3/8", dinner, $14; cup, $11; saucer, $4. An attractive table setting on a white or light pastel tablecloth.

Amethyst candlesticks, $20. These would provide an accent to the amethyst place setting for a dinner.

Vitrock ("Flower Rim"), Anchor Hocking Co., 1934 to late 1930s. This is a beautiful set in white with floral trim. **Left to right:** plate, 10", dinner, $9; bowl, 7-1/2", cereal, $6; sugar, oval (unique shape), $5; creamer, oval (unique shape), $5; cup, $4; saucer, $3.

DEPRESSION GLASS GIFTWARE

One good thing about the severe Depression was being able to give this beautiful glassware as gifts. Giftware still prevailed in that period and this flashy, mass produced glassware filled this requirement. A brightly colored cake plate, bowl, or pitcher made an impressive and very useful gift. A cocktail shaker with a set of matching glasses on a tray is something anyone would admire. The uniquely styled and brightly colored candy dishes would be something I'd like to receive. The fancy and durable glass bakeware would make the perfect gift. The oval casseroles would be a favorite of mine, or any of the covered glassware for that matter.

I can remember the console sets with the elegant candle holders designed in the "modern art style" of the 1930s. These sets were given as wedding gifts. What a magnificent gift to receive.

Relish dishes, tidbits, bon bons, and even dresser sets in a multitude of shapes, sizes, colors, and patterns were also available as gifts.

Smoking was considered fashionable in those days and this resulted in a variety of glass cigarette cases, complete sets on a tray, and of course ash trays. Pink and green ash trays as well as crystal were produced with the dinnerware sets. The ash trays came in the shapes of square, round, hearts, spades, diamonds, and clubs. These were very popular with the people who stayed home and played bridge—one form of entertainment used to amuse themselves with so little available and affordable. Ash trays came in boxes, usually four to constitute a set. Animal ash trays made by L.E. Smith and Company in the 1930s were popular.

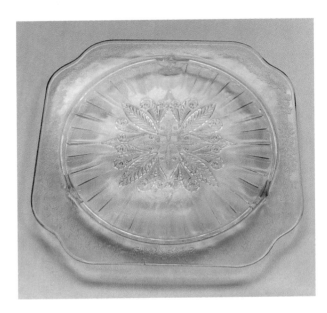

Adam, Jeannette Glass Co., 1932-1934. A beautiful pattern with the center of a group of alternating feathers and plumes and wide radial ridges and rims. Cake plate, 10", ftd., pink, $28.

There were even gifts for men. Sets of whiskey tumblers came with matching trays. For special events like anniversaries there were glass sets decorated with silver and gold. Special sets of coasters as well as coaster and ash tray combinations were lovely gifts. Some of the patterns had these included.

Yes, there was an enormous variety of gift items made in mass-produced glass during the Depression. Many of these were premium items, too. Collectors are just now beginning to realize how much fun it is to collect them. Every color used for the tableware was also used for gift items.

For birthdays, anniversaries, and holidays, I always include a piece of Depression Glass for my friends and family members in their favorite colors and patterns. They really seem to cherish these gifts.

Cherry Blossom, Jeannette Glass Co., 1930-1939. This is a true Depression mold etched pattern in an opaque glass color with a profuse floral all over pattern (AOP). Bowl, berry, 8-1/2", large, $50. An attractive gift to receive.

Cherry Blossom, Jeannette Glass Co., 1930-1939. A very attractive pitcher in green, ftd., 36 oz., 6-3/4", scalloped, $60. Also makes a beautiful gift.

Floral, "Poinsettia," Jeannette Glass Co., 1931-1935. A very attractive pattern in the floral design, resembling a poinsettia with pointed leaves. Pitcher, 8", 32 oz., cone, ftd., $38.

Below:
Ribbon, Hazel Atlas Glass Co., 1930-1932. A pressed pattern which is quite decorated and very representative of the time in which it was made. The bottom is a sunburst of radial lines beginning at the center with every two lines joining in a curved design. The borders resemble lined hairpins. Candy dish and cover, green, $40.

Oyster and Pearl, Anchor Hocking Glass Co., 1938-1940. Console set in crystal, very striking in this pattern. Bowl, 10-1/2", deep, $25; candleholders, 3-1/2", $25 pr.

"Fire-King" Oven Glass, Anchor Hocking Glass Co., blue, 1940s. This is a popular Depression Glass kitchen pattern with a sizable variety of versatile items. They are very desirable collectibles and the market is strong. Prices are increasing. **Center:** pie plate, 9", $10. **Top row left to right:** custard cup, 6 oz., $5 (two styles); baker, 1 pint, $7.

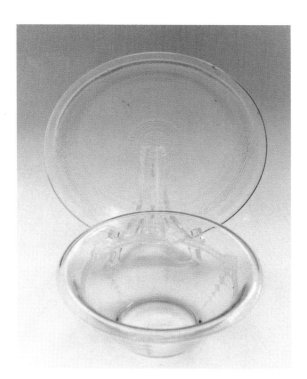

"Fire-King" Oven Glass, Anchor Hocking Glass Co., blue, 1940s. **Top:** pie plate, 8-3/8", $9. **Bottom:** bowl, 6-7/8", utility, $12.50. Very practical gifts.

Vanity tray, Paden City Glass Mfg. Co., Paden City, West Virginia, 1930s. Tray, 12", ftd., elegant frosted with swirled edge, $10-$12. Very popular as a gift.

Smoking Accessories. **Top row:** cigarette holder, decorated in a flower design in pink, produced in the 1930s by New Martinsville, West Virginia, $10-$12. A very convenient gift for storing cigarette packages. **Bottom row left to right:** ash tray produced by Jeannette Glass Co., late 1920s, called Sunflower. A rare piece with the stylized sunflower enclosed by plain undecorated glass in green, 5", $12; Candlewick ash tray in yellow, part of a set in an elegant style, produced by the Imperial Glass Co. 1936-1984, $10; Sunflower ash tray in pink, 5", $9.

Ash tray Set in various colors in a chrome handled container, $10. Produced in the 1930s by New Martinsville, West Virginia. Makes a compact and attractive gift.

Ash trays. **Left to right:** Queen Mary (Prismatic Line), "Vertical Ribbed," Anchor Hocking Glass Co., 1936-1949, ash tray, 3-1/2", round, $3. Waterford "Waffle," Hocking Glass Co., 1938-1944, ash tray, 4", $7.50.

Set of ash trays, Sandwich, Indiana Glass Co., 1920s to 1980s. **Left to right shapes:** spade, $3.50; club, $3.50; heart, $3.50.

Set of whiskey tumblers in silver and gold trim, 1-3/4 oz., $1.50-$3. Very popular in the 1930s. Morgantown, West Virginia was a big producer of liquor glasses and decanter sets.

An array of colored and uniquely handled 1 oz. liquor glasses, $1.50-$3. Produced by Morgantown Glass Works, Morgantown, West Virginia.

A display of colored, 1-3/4 oz. decanter, low and footed glasses, $1.50-$3. Produced in the 1930s by New Martinsville, West Virginia.

An array of coasters. **Top:** crystal, 4", 1930s, $3.50. **Bottom left to right:** Manhattan, 3-1/2", $15 (scarce); iridescent, 4", late 1930s, $4; crystal, late 1930s, $3.50.

WHAT COLLECTORS SHOULD KNOW

Glass collectors are always curious as to the genesis of the finished piece. They want a comprehensive background of the glassware they are collecting, and this is what I have tried to provide in the first two chapters and throughout this book. As I mentioned previously, you have to know more than just the value of the glassware.

There seems to be more collectors of glass than almost anything else. It is therefore highly significant to do your research and observation. I can't reiterate this enough.

With production of this glassware spanning twenty years, thousands of different objects were made in more than one color and pattern. There were many companies that specialized in larger pieces like console sets, salad and fruit bowls, punch bowls, cookie jars, butter tubs, chop plates, grill plates, sandwich servers, relish trays, and tidbits—two tier or three tier. You need to become familiar with all of these in collecting this glassware.

To become a knowledgeable collector, check reference books, price guides, and collecting periodicals at your local library. Subscribe to a monthly newsletter, such as *The Daze, Kovel's,* etc. The information in these are very informative for the novice and advanced collector.

Another interesting and enjoyable way to become more knowledgeable and familiarize yourself with the value of your collection is to join collectors' clubs. Bring your pieces to the meetings and your audience will be very interested to analyze and appraise them. Clubs can be organized by your collector friends or by dealers. Check the antique stores, attend the shows, and express your interest in collecting. This can be a great way to communicate with other collectors and gain invaluable information. There is an increasing interest in these clubs and they are gaining in popularity.

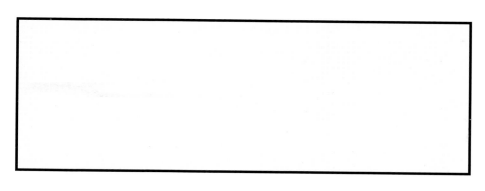

Visit collectible shows, where you will find many experts who will share their knowledge with you. Seek out the dealer who has the collectible category you have. A knowledgeable dealer can give you an accurate description and appraisal of your Depression Glass.

There are also appraisers available who will give you a detailed and written description of the items you have plus their estimated value. Appraisers may require a small fee or may charge nothing.

If interested in selling your products, be realistic about the prices, especially the published values-retail prices, not the price you can sell it for. Sometimes you can sell a piece for 35 to 40 percent more, depending on the rarity and demand. Remember, rarity does determine price, but demand plays a big part, too. If something is priced exorbitantly, pass it up unless you know the value.

Be a wary collector, which begins by being a conservative collector. Research and observation are the key words. Most collectors do not collect indiscriminately. Whatever you decide to collect will depend upon your finances, storage availability, display space, your personal preferences, and investment purposes. Ideal to find are pieces of glassware stored in their original boxes, some still with the label.

The collector who knows his patterns, colors, and values can still be lucky in finding a good supply of choice glassware at bargain prices. With the current rage in collecting, you must be knowledgeable about these facts.

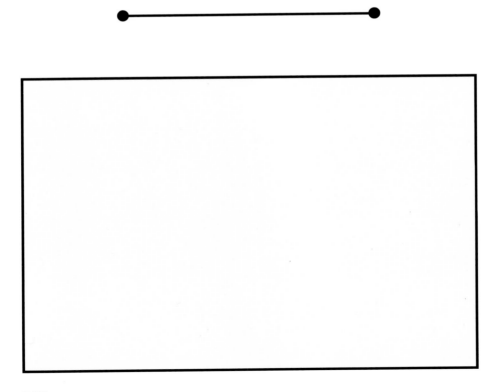

UPDATE ON REPRODUCTIONS

There is still much concern about reproductions and fakes—so much of it creates a great deal of confusion. We collectors are finding this out, and must face the fact that Depression Glass is being produced in the old and some new colors. Reproductions are on the rise. For example:

Miss America, a star pattern, is being reproduced in cobalt blue. This is not an original color, which doesn't create a problem.

Cherry Blossom has been reproduced in the butter dish. This can be easily recognized because it has just one band on the edge of the top. The originals have two.

Thistle pattern is being reproduced in pink, but check color and design carefully.

Another pattern, Cameo, is reproduced in cobalt. Again this color was never used in the original pattern.

A great many reproductions have been made honestly for honest distribution to people who cannot afford the genuine old pieces. Some say there is nothing wrong with buying these pieces so long as they are acknowledged to be what they are, reproductions. To me, however, there is the strong belief that they are not genuine and thus sincere collectors have become victimized.

Collectors, be very cautious and stick to knowledgeable and reputable dealers. They should have the current information on reproductions. If I am not too certain about an item, I will ask the dealer and I usually get an honest answer. I value their integrity. Sometimes an item looks so attractive that we are tempted to buy it, but do not be deceived.

Education has helped considerably in the field of reproductions. I sincerely believe it is much wiser to become extremely knowledgeable about reproductions because in the long run it is more rewarding to possess the genuine article.

Remember, glass that appeals to the collector will always attract a copyist.

Shirley Temple pitchers and mugs, for instance, have been reproduced. The color blue is good but the decal or transfer is something else. It appears shiny with larger dots than the old. Beware! Know the dealer. The old adage holds true, "to know what's old is to know what's new."

Searching for new patterns, I came across this 6" footed relish bowl in the beautiful pattern, "Avocado" No. 61, "Sweet Pear." Actually this was the first piece I had seen in this pattern, and finding it in pink caught my eye. I scrutinized the piece thoroughly and then the color drew my attention. The pink, so delicate and light, made me think this was not a reproduction. I had recently read that this pattern is being reproduced in the color pink, but the new pink has more of an orangish hue. With that information, I knew this color was the original pink. Another factor that made me cautious about deeming the bowl an original was the cheap price. We must consider this factor, too. Perhaps the dealer wasn't sure of the product and therefore priced it accordingly. I guess you could call this one of my "steals." It also proves we must become very familiar with the repros. For your information, this pattern is also produced in green and yellow.

Avocado, "Sweet Pear," No. 601, Indiana Glass Co., 1923-1933. A very attractive pattern and highly collectible in spite of the reproductions. Not so plentiful and therefore expensive. Bowl, 6", relish, ftd., pink, $25, *original* (my steal at $3).

ESSENTIAL COLLECTOR'S VOCABULARY LIST

Depression Glass provides a new and enriched vocabulary for the collector. This terminology is imperative not only for proper identification and background history of this glassware, but for understanding the value as well. Every collector must have a thorough knowledge of the pieces being collected. So many of these words are unfamiliar to even veteran collectors and especially to novice collectors.

Listed below are some of the most common and significant Depression Glass terms.

Amethyst: a light pastel purple.
Amber: a brownish-yellow color.
AOP: an abbreviation for an "all over pattern."
Art Deco: name given to decorative art style of the late 1920s and 1930s.

Berry bowl: a small bowl, usually 3" to 4", used for serving fruits, sauces, and desserts. The large bowl is called the master bowl.
Beverage set: pitcher and set of tumblers, usually 6-8, for serving water, lemonade, or other drinks.
Bon-bon: a small, uncovered candy dish.
Bread and butter plate: a 6" plate for bread and butter.
Bride's basket: an art-glass bowl in a silver-plated stand or frame used for display around 1900.
Burgandy: dark amethyst color, name used by Hazel Atlas Company.
Butter ball or confectioner's dish: a tiny glass plate used for serving, or a shallow glass which has a long center pole with closed handles on top.
Butter dish: a covered dish, round or rectangular, that held butter on the table.

Cake plate: a large flat plate with three short legs.
Camphor glass: frosted glass.
Candelabrum: a candlestick lamp stand, or chandelier with two or more branches.
Candy jar: a dish, usually footed and stemmed, for serving sweets. Made with a knobbed lid and found in dinnerware patterns.
Carafe: a bottle used for serving wine or water.
Cheese dish: similar to covered butter dish with the bottom usually flatter.
Chinex: opaque, ivory colored glass made in the late 1930s and early 1940s by MacBeth Evans.
Chipped-mold process: manner of cutting design directly into surface of the mold by use of tools.
Chop plate: a large serving plate.

Claret: a stemmed glass for serving claret wine.

Closed handles: solid tab handles.

Coaster: a glass liner sometimes used as an ash tray.

Cobalt blue: a dark, deep blue color.

Comport: a long stemmed dish for candy, fruit, etc.

Concentric rings: circles within circles.

Console bowl: a round bowl about 10-12" wide. This was produced with a matching pair of candlesticks so the set could be used in the center of the long table.

Crackle glass: glassware with a surface resembling cracked ice.

Cream soup: a two-handled soup dish.

Cremax: name used by MacBeth Evans for its beige opaque glass resembling China.

Crimped: a pinching effect on the top of a bowl or other dish.

Crystal: clear uncolored glass.

Delphite: light medium blue opaque glassware or blue milk glass.

Demitasse: a smaller than normal cup with saucer.

Dinner set: complete table setting of large plates 9", bowls, cup and saucer, sugar, creamer, salt and pepper shakers, butter dish, candlesticks, coaster, and ash trays.

Domino tray: usually a square, tray-like piece made to hold the cream pitcher with the center ring surrounded by domino sugar cubes.

Ebony: a black color.

Epergne: an elaborate, tiered centerpiece consisting of a metal frame with dishes, vases, or candleholders made of glass, silver, or porcelain made to hold ivy or flowers.

Etched: a design cut into the glass with acid.

Fire King: oven proof glassware name used by Anchor Hocking.

Fired-on: color applied and baked on dish.

Floragold: sprayed iridescent color by Jeannette.

Fluted: a scalloped edge.

Frog: a heavy glass with holes for holding flowers.

Frosted glass: glass given acid spray to acquire roughened translucent appearance.

Goblet: a drinking glass with a stem.

Gravy boat: an oval shaped bowl with a spout for serving gravy.

Grill plate: a divided plate, usually large, introduced during the 1930s.

Hot plate: a glass plate used for protecting hot items placed on the table.

Ice lip: lip of beverage pitcher that is folded inward to catch ice cubes when pouring drinks. Formed by hand, even on Depression Glass.

Ivory: creamy opaque glass.

Jade green: opaque green glass.
Jadeite: an opaque, light green color.
Jug: used interchangeably with pitcher.

Luncheon plate: an 8" or 9" plate, smaller than a dinner plate.
Luncheon set: table service not including the large 9" plate, fewer shapes.

Mayonnaise bowl: an open, cone shaped comport.
Milk glass: white opaque glass, usually heavy.
Mint: this is a common word any Depression Glass collector will hear over and over again. It refers to a perfect, undamaged item with no scratches that looks as if it came from a store. If an item is in the original box, that definitely adds to its value. This is known as "mint in the box" and is the best a collector can hope for.
Mold etched: Process of etching a pattern into the mold by a series of wax transfers and acid baths to achieve the effect of etching through raised designs on the outer surface of the finished glass product.
Monax: a white color.
Motif: the design on the glass.

Nappy: a round or oval dish with a flat bottom and sloping sides, about 6" in diameter. An all-purpose dish used for puddings, ice cream, peas, apple sauce, or other juicy foods.

Opalescent: showing a display of colors like that of an opal.

Parfait: a tall ice cream dish used for sundaes in soda fountains.
Paste-mold: mold kept at a continually high temperature throughout the molding process and then intermittently cooled. Used infrequently on Depression Glass.
Platonite: opaque white glass made by Hazel Atlas Company, sometimes with fired on colors.
Platter: an oval or oblong shaped meat platter.
Premium glassware: tableware and other pieces in Depression Glassware made as promotional items or giveaways by businesses and services during the Depression era.
Pressed mold: molds used or made by forming around a wood model and given no further embellishment.
Pyrex: heat resistant glassware for cooking utensils made by Corning. This word has become generic and now is used to describe all heat-resistant glass utensils.

Rayed: spoke-like designs on glass bottoms.
Reissue: to issue again.
Relish dish: an oblong pickle dish.
Reproduction: a likeness.
Reproduce: cause to exist again.
Rose bowl: a small, curved-in edged bowl.

Ruby flashed: process of covering surface or parts of surface of crystal glass with red coating in imitation of Bohemian glass of earlier period.

Ruby red: cherry red color.

Salad bowl: a 7" to 7-1/2" plate for serving salads.

Salad set: set of glassware consisting of a large bowl and 6 or 8 nappies, plates around 8" sometimes included.

Salver: a round tray or platter on a high stem used for serving desserts or tea sandwiches.

Sandwich server: a center handled serving plate, or a salver.

Sherbet: a small, usually footed dessert dish.

Smoke: monax opaque glass by MacBeth Evans with gray trims.

Spoon holder: a vase-like container used to hold spoons on the dining table.

Stemmed glasses: there are special names for stemmed glasses of various sizes and shapes; cordial, wine, claret, champagne, and water.

Table set: a matching sugar bowl, creamer, spoon holder, and butter dish.

Tid bit: a two or three layer serving piece with a metal upright and handle. Also called an hors-d'oeurves plate or a cookie plate.

Topaz: a bright yellow color.

Trivet: a three-footed hot plate.

Tumbler: a drinking glass with no stem.

Ultra-marine: a blue-green color.

Vitrock: white opaque unglazed glass made by Hocking Glass Company.

Water set: a pitcher with tumblers and sometimes a matching tray in cut or pressed glass.

Wine set: a decanter with matching wine glasses.

COMPANIES COLLECTORS SHOULD KNOW

Many companies produced Depression Glass. Some were more popular than others, producing in large quantities. The process of setting up the plants for the production of tank glass was very expensive. Smaller glass companies had a difficult time competing with the larger ones, especially during the Great Depression. Some glass firms already had a good start in the production of the tank glass pieces when the Depression took place.

The popular companies that collectors are more familiar with and that produced most of the Depression Glass are listed below in alphabetical order.

Anchor Hocking Glass Company of Lancaster, Ohio (early 1920s-1938). This company was the largest producer of dinner tableware. Large catalogue and chain stores were supplied with glassware by this company. Their designs ran the gamut from traditional sandwich type to 1930s modern.

Federal Glass Company of Columbus, Ohio (1933-1937). The major patterns collected today can be attributed to Federal. This company produced an enormous amount of Depression Glass in machine pressed and mold-etched dinnerware in the popular array of colors.

Hazel Atlas Company of Clarksville, West Virginia (early 1930s). Much of the glass tableware and glass kitchenware that is collected today from the 1920s and 1930s was produced by this company. Tumblers were produced in such abundance that the Clarksburg, West Virginia plant became known as the "World's Famous and Biggest Tumbler Factory."

Indiana Glass Company of Dunkirk, Indiana (1926-1931). This company identified their patterns with numbers rather than names. They produced a number of mold-etched patterns in the early 1920s and pressed glass tableware into the 1930s. Their serviceable crystal ware produced for the soda fountains and tearooms in the 1920s and 1930s is highly collectible.

Jeannette Glass Company of Jeannette, Pennsylvania (1935-1938). This company will always be remembered by all collectors for their exquisite mold-etched patterns and the typical Depression colors. The modern designs of the decorative and artistic style as well as traditional shapes were typical of this company.

MacBeth Glass Company of Charlerol, Pennsylvania (1930-1932). Produced five of the major collectible Depression Glass tableware patterns that were so popular. Produced much of the pink and daintier patterns.

Other familiar companies producing less quantities but beautiful glassware are listed below in alphabetical order.

Bartlett-Collins (1931). Produced utilitarian pressed table items, like versatile serving pieces including decorated water sets, fruit bowls, console sets, sandwich trays, vases, and comports. Best known for its kitchen lamps.

Cambridge of Cambridge, Ohio (1920s-1930s). Famous as the largest producer of American glass. Labeled as the champion of color; quality of glass was superb.

Diamond Glassware Company of Indiana, Pennsylvania (1920s-1930s). Produced a high grade of decorated tableware and special novelties. Brought out the deep red glass in 1924 along with the other colors: amethyst and ritz blue. Black was Diamond's foremost color with gold and silver trims.

Duncan and Miller Glass Company of Washington, Pennsylvania (1936-1955). This company is best known for its pattern glass and the re-creation of the Sandwich pattern. Also famous for the crystal in the elegant line and for the swans.

Fenton of Williamstown, West Virginia (1920s to present). Their glass making plant distinguished their name for decades. Instrumental in developing the iridescent colored ware. This is carnival glass, collected today. Their line of glassware in all of the transparent colors and shapes was most representative of the Depression Era.

Fostoria Glass Company (1915-1986). This company became the largest producer of quality glassware. All of their glassware was very distinctive, brilliant, and highly collectible, and the colorful patterns of the Depression Era are highly treasured.

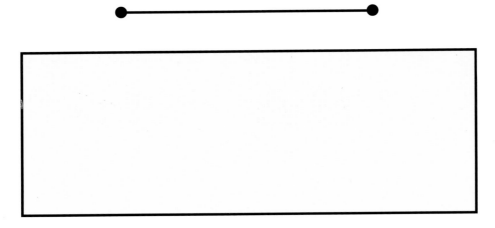

Heisey Company of Newark, Ohio (1920s-1985). Produced an abundant supply of handmade glass which became highly popular. Collectors search for the quality and vivid colors that it produced.

Imperial Company of Bellaire, Ohio (1920-1928). This glassware brought out the color with all its brilliance. The popular luncheon sets were produced by the thousands. Imitation cut glass (called Nu-Cut) in crystal and transparent colors was produced in the 1920s.

L.E. Smith of Mt. Pleasant, Pennsylvania (1920s-1934). This company is remembered mainly for the black glass, a collector's dream. It also produced glassware in all of the Depression colors in the 1920s and was instrumental in kitchen items.

Libby Glass Company (1920s-1930s). This company has a long history but in the '20s and '30s it brought out color and novel designs. It became famous for a variety of tumblers. It also produced the characteristic Depression Era colors and created fine cuttings and artistic quality in glassware.

McKee Glass Company of Jeannette, Pennsylvania (1923-1930). This company was famous for the production of much of the kitchenware items. Also popular for opaque wares, Sunkist reamers, and children's sets, it brought forth glass products of almost every description.

New Martinsville of West Virginia (1923-1930s). This company was noted for novel designs in the popular colors and produced almost any item, even liquor sets despite the prohibition times.

Westmoreland Company, Grapefield, Pennsylvania (1920s-1985). Produced specialties at first, but in the 1920s glassware of high quality was produced. Early American patterns were recreated and the production of milk glass began. This is still very popular today.

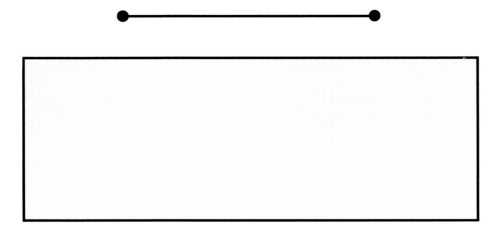

WHY I'M STILL ADDICTED TO COLLECTING DEPRESSION GLASS

The memories of Depression Glass from my youth will never fade away. Part of my interest in collecting Depression Glass is sentimental. The treasured items passed from grandmother to mother to daughter have great sentimental value, regardless of their intrinsic worth, and should not be relegated to storage or ignored. I have heard many stories about storing boxes of this colored glassware in barns or sheds, or even discarding it.

I can still recall memories of my grandmother's house filled with the pink and green glassware. Today, I refer to this as "grandma's glass."

The premium giveaways still intrigue me. Receiving the various pieces and then building sets of this beautiful glassware for dinnerware of the time will always be remembered.

Again, the rainbow of colors and the indescribable, numerous patterns are the strong factors in my continued collecting.

The hunt for the missing pieces in my various sets and for rare pieces is now my goal. Rare pieces are very marketable, and a challenge to find. There's always a "sleeper" in these patterns and finding it is the big thrill. Assembling the various sets, enjoying them, and passing them on to my family as treasured heirlooms is my desire.

The collecting instinct has always abided in me, as is typical of nearly everyone. We all have the urge to collect antique or modern items. This often begins in childhood, continues throughout the teen and middle age life, and then blossoms in full in the later years, leading to a full time hobby, career, or business. As my husband and I have found out, our retirement years have been so fulfilling and lively collecting and researching Depression Glass.

To sum up my addiction to this glassware, the veritable array of colors, the endless patterns, sentiments involved, the admiration for this glassware, and the potential investment purposes all contribute to this. My passion for collecting Depression Glass is stronger than ever. I will travel miles when I hear of a sale featuring this glassware. I doubt if I will ever tire of my love for it and the research.

The daily use of this colored glassware is the viewing of the "rainbow colors." Since I started using my glassware, serving my guests, and bringing some of the serving pieces for special occasions, more of my friends are following suit. It's sort of a display and a great conversation piece. Sharing this is another way of becoming more familiar with the numerous patterns. How often have I heard this remark, "Oh, I have that piece or I just saw that not long ago at an antique shop."

Left:
An array of the typical colors and patterns of Depression Glass. **Top row left to right:** Daisy, amber, tumbler, 9 oz., ftd., $18; Cherry Blossom, tray, pink, 10-1/2", sandwich, 2 handled, $30; Ribbon, candy dish and cover, green, $40. **Middle row left to right:** Cameo, "Ballerina," or "Dancing Girl," yellow, cup and saucer, $10; Swirl, "Petal Swirl," ultramarine, bowl, 5-1/4", cereal, $18; Vitrock ("flower rim,"), white, cup and saucer, $6; **Center:** bowl, turquoise blue, 4-1/2", berry, $7.

REMINISCING ABOUT DEPRESSION GLASS

Depression Glass has fascinated many generations. It's like an echo of the past, a luminous symbol of the age shining with the promised prosperity of the '20s and '30s.

Glassware was a big boon or trend for the American home. Very few realize how this machine made, mass produced glassware, so available and cheap, kept the economy going. Carloads of this colored glassware were stored in department stores and then distributed widely. Advertising the colored glassware was phenomenal, stressing that color was right for the tables and that it was durable.

Hard work was the key word for everyone during the Depression Era. The evening meal was the only time the family had for being together after a workday of twelve hours. Colored glassware was dinner time, family together time, and a respite in each day's struggle. What a beautiful display of the table settings, completely coordinated from salt and pepper shakers to dessert dishes.

In many homes, this colored glassware was perhaps the only pretty thing the family owned. Visiting the various homes and seeing all the glassware that each one owned became something of a hobby. The similarity and identity of this glassware brought about a sense of togetherness. The people could relate to all of this, sharing a common bond. Something like this was needed to piece their lives back together during these turbulent years.

Families made memories together and this togetherness helped them weather the tough times during the Depression, which took its toll on many. There were no strokes of good luck or windfalls that would occur, only honest, hard work and frugal spending habits to support a family.

When I see this glittering glassware in my home, it brings back such unforgettable memories. As I use and display this colored glassware, I can't help but reflect how each piece is treasured. This is why I want to pass this on to my generation, so that they too can relate to this inspired glassware that became such a source of historical significance and enlightenment to the people in this depressing era.

Can any product be remembered as well as this colored glassware? It is linked to the most dramatic period of history. It had a definite meaning, a distinct part in the culture of that era.

It is sad to me that this brilliant glassware was not treasured more and considered significant in that initial period. It was just used for everyday glassware, stored away and even discarded. Years later came the awareness that this glassware had a special beauty and history. It had finally been discovered and the years were followed by scores of women and men everywhere becoming collectors of it.

Just recently I talked to an eighty-eight year old woman who had a house loaded with all types of Depression Glass. Not knowing the value of it, she kept giving pieces to her friends, neighbors, and the family members who wanted it. Now, to her dismay, she realized she had a fortune and if she had known then what she knew now, she would never have given it away. Does this story sound familiar? Perhaps too familiar.

As we have become familiar with the background of this tumultuous era which affected nearly every aspect of the society, Depression Glass seems the perfect representative of this period.

Living in this era, I can fully relate to the impact that the Great Depression had in the lives of the people struggling so hard to survive. Looking back on these events and experiencing the good and bad has made me more appreciative of the finer and more conventional ways of living. I have vivid reminders of this colorful and brilliant glassware that became the symbol of hope and light for the majority of the people.

Display of typical Depression Glass colors and patterns. **Top row left to right:** tumbler, red, $20; Jubilee, topaz, tray, 11", 2 handled cake, $45. **Center:** Normandie, "Bouquet and Lattice," sherbet, iridescent, $7; Colony, crystal, candy dish with cover, $45. **Bottom row:** Moroccan, amethyst, cup and saucer, $6; Aurora, cobalt blue, 5-3/8", $17-$18; Ovide, black, cup and saucer, $10.

BIBLIOGRAPHY

Florence, Gene. *The Collector's Encyclopedia of Depression Glass*. Paducah, KY: Collector Books, 1996.

Huxford, Sharon and Bob. *Schroeder's Antiques Price Guide*. Paducah, KY: Collector Books, 1996.

Klamkin, Marian. *The Collector's Guide to Depression Glass*. The Hawthorne Company, 1974.

Kovel, Ralph and Terry. *Antiques and Collectibles Price List*. New York: Crown Publishers, Inc., 1996.

Rinker, Harry L. *Warman's Antiques and Their Prices*. Radnor, PA: Wallace-Homestead Book Co., 1995.

Steel, Teri, Editor. *The Daze*, monthly newspaper. Otisville, Michigan.

Warner, Ian. *Swanky Swigs: A Pattern Guide and Checklist* (4th Printing). Otisville, Michigan: The Daze, Inc., 1992.

Weatherman, Hazel. *Colored Glassware of the Depression Era 1*. Ozark, Missouri: Weatherman Glassbooks, 1970.

——. *Colored Glassware of the Depression Era 2*. Ozark, Missouri: Weatherman Glassbooks, 1974.